A Millionaire's Notebook
How Ordinary People Can Achieve Extraordinary Success

Steve Scott held and lost nine jobs in his first six years after college. He was told more than once that he would never succeed. Yet this former corporate failure not only became a multimillionaire himself, more than forty others have become millionaires as a result of the efforts and advice of Steve and his partners. Ordinary people just like you, including a housewife, a makeup artist, a hair stylist, a salesman, a teacher, a convenience store clerk, a marriage counsellor, a carpenter, a doctor, a dog trainer, a former P.E. teacher, to name a few.

Not Simply a Book about Making Millions
A Book about Achieving Incredible Degrees of Success!

This book is not a guide to making millions, although its insights and advice could certainly result in that. It's not a book about theories. Instead, it's a step-by-step guide to success—success in any field, at any age. It tracks Steve Scott's life from mediocre high school student to a corporate failure to number-one marketing entrepreneur in the United States. It shows how a "nobody" who couldn't even afford to pay for his first child's birth could create more than a dozen record-breaking companies in completely different industries, selling over one billion dollars in products.

Unlike Any Success or Business Book You've Ever Read!

This book doesn't stop with general principles or psychological motivation, but instead gives specific tasks you can instantly apply to your personal or business life.

Your Personal Notebook for Success

Each chapter ends with a section that leads the reader through a step-by-step process that can result in greater success than he or she has ever experienced. The Notebook for Success provides a guide that can be used by anyone from a high school student to the CEO of a Fortune 500 company. You'll understand why Steve Scott firmly believes that ANYONE can significantly increase his or her "batting averages" in any area of life and break through the barriers that separate mediocrity from phenomenal success—barriers imposed by others or even by ourselves.

If you want to achieve a higher degree of success than you've ever thought possible, this book will become the most important book on success you, your employees, and your children will ever read.

A
Millionaire's
Notebook

HOW ORDINARY PEOPLE CAN ACHIEVE
EXTRAORDINARY SUCCESS

STEVEN K. SCOTT

A FIRESIDE BOOK
PUBLISHED BY SIMON & SCHUSTER
NEW YORK   LONDON   TORONTO   SYDNEY   TOKYO   SINGAPORE

FIRESIDE
Rockefeller Center
1230 Avenue of the Americas
New York, NY 10020

Designed by Chris Welch

Manufactured in the United States of America

7   9   10   8   6

Library of Congress Cataloging-in-Publication Data
Scott, Steve, date.
A millionaire's notebook : how ordinary people
can achieve extraordinary success / Steven K. Scott.
p.   cm.
"A Fireside Book."
1. Telemarketing--United States--Case studies.
2. Television advertising--United States--Case studies.
3. Success in business--United States--Case studies.   4. Scott, Steve, date
5. Marketing executives--United States--Biography.   I. Title.
HF5415. 1265.S395   1996
650.1--dc20   95-40929
CIP

ISBN 0-684-80303-8

Acknowledgments

This book

Bob Marsh, Gary Smalley, and my wife, Shannon Scott. Without their encouragement this book would have never been started, much less finished.

Jan Miller, my favorite literary agent . . . for all of the faith, encouragement, and help. In all the world, there's only *one* Jan Miller!

Caroline Sutton, Simon & Schuster senior editor, who deserves a series of medals . . . for patience, kindness, enthusiasm, and incredible talent.

Marilyn Abraham, Mark Gompertz, Sue Fleming-Holland, and all of the others at Simon & Schuster who have believed in this project and have made it possible.

Brett Smiley and Tamme Webb for their input at every phase of this project.

Dick Birkey and Nathan Heinze for their cover design.

My Business

Bob Marsh, the most incredible mentor and boss and adopted father a young man could ever hope for.

My partners John Marsh, David Marsh, Ed Shipley, Ben Weaver, Jeff Heft, and Jim Shaughnessy . . . the most awesome partners and best friends ever to build a group of businesses.

The late Michael Landon . . . an incredible friend and believer in Steve Scott and ATC. You are irreplaceable and terribly missed.

Frank Kovacs, my right and left arms, without whom I would never want to produce a single show.

Dana Jack, my favorite video editor . . . by a million miles!

Patty Brenner, my marketing right arm.

All of ATC's wonderful employees who make ATC the most productive company in America.

All of the television and film crew members who make my shoots run like clockwork and give me such beautiful footage to work with.

Rich Hersh, the best commercial deal maker in Hollywood.

Brian Dubin, the best commercial deal maker in New York.

Mike Siegal, for giving me the chance to come up to the plate in the bottom of the ninth with two men out and three men on.

Pat Boone, for taking a risk with ATC before anybody in the world knew who we were.

Harry Morgan, for all your help when things looked pretty hopeless.

Gary West, for your lifetime help in our business and for the lifeline you threw us in 1985.

Dr. Roy Campbell and Dr. Louis Grossman, my most inspirational and motivational marketing professors at Arizona State University.

Marlene Delnoce, for all of her input on my scripts and ideas for the past twenty years.

Tom Delnoce, of West America, Scottsdale, Arizona, for doing such an incredible job with all of my investments during the past twenty years . . . in my opinion, the best financial adviser in the world.

In memory of Gordon Scott 1915–1995

Decorated World War II combat pilot, traffic safety innovator, and the most wonderful father a son could ever have.

Dedicated to my mother, Minnie Aiton Scott, whose boundless love has filled the lives of everyone she has ever known. To my wife and children, who have made life worth living; and to my partners, who have made twenty years of work outrageously fun and incredibly profitable.

Contents

Why Would the Marketing Man Behind America's Most Productive Company Reveal the Secrets of His Success?

What this book is about, why it was written, and how it can change your life and the lives of those you love.

How does a failure and corporate dropout (who in his first six years after college held nine different jobs, earning at best $1,500 a month) become a multimillionaire earning more per year than 492 of the 500 CEOs who head the Fortune 500 Companies? How does someone who was told by his corporate bosses that he would never succeed in marketing become America's single most successful consumer marketing expert? And how does the obscure little company he owns with six partners become the most productive company in America? It wasn't luck and it wasn't genius. It was the implementation of a series of specific steps that resulted in unimaginable success!

The purpose of this book is to give you a set of very specific insights, laws of success, and steps of action that you or anyone you love can use to achieve degrees of success that would otherwise be highly unlikely or impossible for you to attain. Whether you're a high school student, a homemaker, or the CEO of a Fortune 500 company, if you apply what you learn from this book, you will achieve degrees of success that are greater than you might imagine.

You'll learn that past achievement or failure is *not* a true predictor of the future. You'll learn that if you can do one thing well, you have a genuine potential for extraordinary success. You'll discover two factors that are far more important to your future than your credentials or resume. You'll encounter insights, principles, and specific steps to success so vividly demonstrated that you'll never forget them. And most important, you'll find at the end of every chapter a step-by-step interactive guide that will enable you to *instantly* achieve greater success in your own career. In other words, if success for you lies on top of a ten-foot wall, this book will provide the ladder to climb it, one step at a time. Remember, anyone can climb a ten-foot wall with a sixteen-foot ladder.

After twenty years of watching these steps work over and over again, I decided it was time to "go public," to share them with the millions of other men and women, young and old, who, like me, think of themselves as ordinary and average but, unlike me, have *not* discovered that ordinary people can attain extraordinary success.

It's not a matter of luck—you don't have to wait to win the lottery. It's not a matter of education—you don't have to get an MBA from Harvard. It's not even a matter of "positive thinking." (If success were simply a matter of positive thinking, every person who ever got his or her real estate license or joined a multilevel sales organization would be a multimillionaire.) What is true is that achievement in every realm and at every level is the result of specific steps that a person has taken to bring him to his or her goal.

An airline crew doesn't take off from Kennedy Airport in New York and arrive in Los Angeles because it got lucky or because they are geniuses or kept telling themselves, "We think we can, we think we can, we think we can." They get from point A to point B every time they take off because they take specific steps and follow a set of navigational charts and aeronautical procedures from takeoff to landing.

Which of the following categories describes your current status?

1. High school student
2. College student
3. Homemaker
4. Out of work—age 17 to 22
5. Out of work—age 23 to 45
6. Out of work—age 46 to 55
7. Out of work—age 56 +
8. Self-employed
9. Blue-collar worker
10. White-collar worker
11. Lower management in a corporation
12. Middle management in a corporation
13. Upper management in a corporation
14. Business owner

If you are in any of the above categories, the specific steps you learn in this book will equip you to attain what would otherwise seem unattainable. "Wait a minute," you say. "Who isn't included in one of these categories?" You're right, and that is just my point. I have been in eleven of these fourteen categories at different times in my life, and these steps have worked in every one of them. As for the three categories that don't apply to me—3, 6, and 7—they have been successfully navigated by others I've known who have also used these steps.

If this sounds like the kind of hype you've read in other motivational books, I apologize, but this time it's *not* hype. I'm not a professor or a motivational speaker. I don't make a living by telling others how to succeed. But along with my partners, in 1976 I used the steps you're going to read about to start a marketing company with less than $5,000 and built it into the most successful company in its field, with sales of more than $230 million in 1994—all without using a dime of public money and without building a huge organization with enormous overhead.

Whenever I meet people, they inevitably ask what I do. As soon as I tell them, they usually want to know everything about my work, my company, and how it all came to be. It's an enjoyable and unusual story. After all, how often do you hear about a group of guys with no experience coming together, having a ball, and building the most productive business in America?

Forbes magazine defines productivity as "the amount of profit a company makes per company employee." In 1992, *Forbes* called King World, the syndicators of the *Oprah, Jeopardy!* and *Wheel of Fortune* television shows, the most productive company in America. Our company is privately held by seven partners and was therefore not included in their report. Had they known our numbers, we would have been rated number one. Our profit per employee was more than double *Forbes*'s number one pick. In terms of profitability as a percentage of sales, we not only lead our industry but our percentage of profit is more than double that of the top ten retailers in America, and more than double any mail-order company or TV shopping network in America.

When I first decided to share our insights and steps to success in a book, I had to decide whether to enumerate and amplify them in a dry "how-to" format or use my story and the story of our business as a means of demonstrating these principles and steps. I chose to use the latter format because it's a lot more entertaining and therefore more likely to be read, start to finish, and because our story focuses on how average, inexperienced people can achieve unimaginable success.

My six partners and I own and manage American Telecast Corporation (ATC) and its sister companies. You've never heard of us or our privately held company because we've never spent a dime to promote our name. And yet you've seen our commercials and infomercials, and the odds are that either you or someone you're close to has purchased our products. Some of our companies, products, and spokespersons are as follows:

COMPANY	PRODUCT	SPOKESPERSON
Westgate Fitness Inc.	Treadmills	Jane Fonda
Gary Smalley Seminars	Relationship videos	Kathie Lee and Frank Gifford, Connie Sellecca and John Tesh
Luxurious Hair, Ltd.	Hair extensions	Priscilla Presley
Lori Davis Hair	Hair care products	Cher
Cher Beauty Products	Skin care products	Cher
Deal-A-Meal Corp.	Weight loss products	Richard Simmons
Victoria Jackson Cosmetics	Cosmetics	Ali MacGraw, Lisa Hartman, Meredith Baxter
Where There's a Will There's an "A"	Educational videos	John Ritter, Michael Landon
Wally Armstrong Golf	Golf videos	Kenny Rogers and Pat Summerall
The World of Peter Rabbit	Children's videos	Angela Lansbury

In May 1976, Bob Marsh, founder of American Telecast Corporation and my mentor, recruited me to join him in starting a TV mail-order marketing company. The first two-minute commercial that sold our first product cost $4,200 to produce and generated $20 million in sales for our new company. In the years that followed we pioneered new ways to market goods and services directly to the consumer through two-minute television commercials, setting records in nearly every industry we entered, including cosmetics, publishing, telephone products, and life and health insurance, to name a few. But as good as those early days were, the real launching pad of our current success began in 1987 with the airing of our first half-hour television "infomercial." From that first airing we have been considered the industry leader in terms of both sales and profits.

From the first day of our business my role has been to work on our marketing strategies and to write and produce our commercials and infomercials, which have generated more than 20 million phone orders and more than $1 billion in sales. The vast majority of those sales have occurred during the past seven years. I've enjoyed an 83 percent success rate, compared to an industry success rate of less than 1 percent. (I define "success rate" as the percentage of infomercials produced that are actually rolled out into a national television campaign and produce a seven figure profit.) Of the twenty-four infomercials I've written and produced, twenty have been rolled out into national campaigns, each creating millions of dollars in profits.

During the last twenty years I have had the privilege (and in some cases the pain) of directing more major entertainment celebrities than have appeared in all of the other national commercials produced by all of the advertising agencies in America during the same time period.

This background is given to you not to be boastful but to show you how someone with no more intelligence or talent than you have can achieve incredible degrees of success. In fact, if anything, you'll discover that your qualifications and potential for success are greater than mine were when we started our business.

This book will give you what I believe are the keys to my success and the success of our company. But far more important, it will show you step by step how you can use what I've learned to achieve more success (and have fun doing it) than you might think possible. So let's get to the good stuff.

By the way, at the end of each chapter is a section entitled "Notebook for Success." It includes a quick review of the insights and laws of success discussed in the chapter. It also provides projects for readers who want to see incredible improvement in their success batting averages, projects that provide step-by-step guides for significantly increasing success.

CHAPTER 1

Steven Who?

Even if You Weren't Popular in High School, Didn't Make Straight A's, and Didn't Make the Football Team, You Can <u>Still</u> Achieve Phenomenal Success

Two Stevens sat next to each other at high school football games; one was in the band, the other in the color guard. Both were mediocre students, rarely dated, and were totally unknown. They excelled in nothing significant. One was Steven Spielberg, and the other was Steven who?

INSIGHT 1: PAST ACHIEVEMENT IS <u>NOT</u> A TRUE PREDICTOR OF FUTURE SUCCESS

Most high schools save a part of their yearbook for the "most likely" selections. You know—the student most likely to succeed, the student most likely to be president, and so forth. I remember voting that Chuck James would be the most likely to succeed. He was senior class president, an "A" student, a good athlete, and very popular. I remember when the ballots were passed out to the senior class. There were many categories, and many students were nominated for each category. Obviously, my name was not on the ballot. If it had been, I definitely wouldn't have won in any category. Most of the class of 1966 would have had puzzled looks on their faces and would have had one question when they came to my name: "Steven who?"

I didn't have the looks or athletic prowess to be popular with the "in" crowd, and my "B" average wasn't high enough to put me in the intellectual crowd. Consequently, most of my friendships were with kids off campus. As a freshman I joined the Civil Air Patrol because two of my buddies had joined. Even though I didn't realize it at the time, joining CAP was going to play a very important role in my future.

Another Steven at our school was very similar to me. Like me, he didn't have the looks or athletic abilities to be part of the "in" crowd. He was a mediocre student, and his favorite activities were likewise "off campus." He was a good clarinetist, however, and was in the school's marching band. But at school football games, nothing was better than being on the football team. They had it made. And nothing was worse (in terms of status) than being in the band—nothing except being in the color guard. Teenagers in the 60s weren't impressed with high school students who wore military uniforms. But we got free tickets to the games and sat next to the band. I sat next to the clarinets and often conversed with the clarinetist who sat on my right. His name was the same as mine (Steve), but that was all I knew about him.

Twenty years later I received a call from my mom asking if I had ever met Steven Spielberg when I was at Arcadia. I told her he couldn't have been a student at Arcadia because even though most kids didn't know me, I knew just about everyone and never met him. She told me to grab my yearbook and look up his name. I not only found his name, I found his picture and was amazed to discover he was the "Steve" I sat next to at so many football games!

How could this be? How could Steven Spielberg have gone to my high school and yet have been totally unknown to me and most of the other students on campus? Surely his genius, his creativity, his incredible drive would have been evident to all, even in high school. Not even close. And yet all the qualities that have made him so successful were just as much alive in his mind and heart then. So why was he never successful in anything significant in high school? The answer lies in what we deem "significant."

In school the three most important areas of achievement are athletics, grades, and popularity—at least those are the three most significant areas to students and teachers. So when a person doesn't excel in any one of those areas, he doesn't excel in anything "significant." By academia's definition, neither Steven nor I excelled in anything that mattered, and I'm sure none of our peers or faculty ever expected us to achieve anything noteworthy with our lives.

This is the kind of narrow outlook that traps probably 90 percent of the American population; that is, most of us never achieve stardom in school, so when we pass into adulthood, we never expect to achieve anything worthwhile in life. We have accepted everyone else's definition of "significance" and consequently set our sights so low that we never even try to achieve the success most of us would like to attain.

I am told that when baby elephants are born, their trainers tie a rope to a pole planted securely in the ground and then tie the other end to the baby elephant. The elephant quickly learns that when that rope is on his neck, he can't go anywhere. By the time he becomes an adult, he can be tied to a small pole that he could easily rip right out of the ground, but he doesn't even try because he has been conditioned to believe that when that rope is around his neck, he can't go anywhere.

The same thing happens with most adult Americans. Having achieved nothing they consider important in their youth, they have come to believe that they are simply average and therefore expect to achieve nothing significant in their lives. By the end of this book I hope that *everybody* reading it will see that the superachievers are no different from the rest of us. They have just learned that the rope that kept them tied to the stake was really only a thread, and the stake itself only a yardstick. By the end of this book, you will have no reason to accept mediocrity. At this point you can't even begin to imagine what average people can do when they break loose of the bonds that have kept them bound to the "status quo."

So the first law of success involves your past and how to break loose from what you see as your *lack* of success.

> *Law of Past Failures: Don't use your past failures or lack of achievement as an excuse or limitation for your lack of achievement in the present or future. The former does not control the latter.*

INSIGHT 2: IF YOU CAN DO ONE THING WELL—EVEN IF IT DOESN'T SEEM SIGNIFICANT—YOU HAVE THE POTENTIAL FOR PHENOMENAL SUCCESS.

Even though Steven Spielberg and I achieved nothing significant in high school, we did achieve some things that seemed *insignificant* to us and to everyone else around us (except our parents).

Steven was an excellent clarinetist and even gained a headline in our yearbook praising him for his acting talent in a school play (although his name was misspelled in the headline). But even more important than his musical or acting talent was his talent in something else: making entertaining home movies with the Super 8 film camera his mother gave him in elementary school. Do you think the faculty or students at Arcadia High even knew about this activity, much less recognized or valued it? I'm sure the faculty never recognized it even though he often cut school specifically to go out and film things. How insignificant was this high school activity of Steven's?

Today, four of the top ten grossing films of all time were directed by Steven Spielberg.

My success was even more mundane than Steven's. My dad had always regretted not learning to type in high school. In his adult years, the fruit of his creative mind was stifled or thwarted over and over again by his inability to type. When I was choosing my electives for my freshman year in high school, he told me I would have to take a year of typing. I argued as hard and as long as I could, but to no avail. In my mind, typing was for girls and I was a teenage boy, and those two thoughts just didn't coincide.

I finally struck a deal with him that both of us could live with. If I could end the semester as the fastest typist in the class, I wouldn't have to take a second semester of typing. By the end of the first semester, I *was* the fastest typist out of about sixty students. Little did I know that typing would become the cornerstone of most of my other achievements in life. Thanks, Dad.

As I mentioned earlier, I joined the Civil Air Patrol my freshman year to be with two of my buddies. The three of us were the only ones out of sixteen hundred students in our high school who were part of this off-campus organization. Certainly this was another "insignificant" part of my teenage years. Right? Wrong! Because I could type, I was quickly promoted over my friends. This was the first success I had tasted since little league baseball, and it tasted wonderful. I began to work harder to fulfill requirements for promotions, and with each promotion the taste grew sweeter and the desire to succeed more consuming.

By the time I was graduated from high school, I was the highest ranking CAP cadet in the state and had won numerous national awards, including flying lessons that enabled me to receive my private pilot's license when I was sixteen.

My achievements in CAP meant nothing to the faculty and students of my high school, but they meant plenty to my future. My achievement in this one area taught me that I could be successful even if the success came in an apparently insignificant endeavor. As a skinny, acne-faced teenager, I gained my first bit of self-respect.

A Special Note to Parents Who Want to See Their Children Learn to Achieve Success

You can help your children break the bonds of mediocrity that school and their peers use to bind them. Children don't have to be a success at everything—or, for that matter, anything significant—as long as they are successful at something.

The key is for you to listen and watch for those things that seem interesting to them. My seven-year-old loves to "build" with Legos, so every time he creates a new structure, I praise him—not just with generalities ("That's a great building") but with meaningful specifics ("I like how you put windows on each side, and I love the roof").

For my nineteen-year-old it's his ability on the drums and guitar. He's totally self-taught. His music is the kind I would never listen to for more than a few minutes, but boy, is he good! And I am *so* proud of him. He is also the best friend any of his friends could ever have, and I praise him for his love and care for them. For my fourteen-year-old it's his poetry and his computer skills. And I praise my twenty-three-year-old's success in her work with high school students. She is a volunteer leader with Young Life, a Christian youth organization, and, to my mind, the best leader her girls could ever have.

I could talk about my kids all day, but they're not the subject of this book—maybe the next one.

As I mentioned earlier, typing was the other "insignificant" thing I was good at. Typing didn't stop being useful to me with my first promotion in CAP. My writing is so sloppy, it was next to impossible for even me to read. To make it legible I had to write very slowly, and because my mind works a lot faster than my right hand, I wasn't very good at any form of written communication until I learned to type.

To my amazement I discovered that I could type almost as fast as I could think. Thus, I could write creatively and persuasively with a typewriter even though that was not the case when I wrote longhand. For me typing has been the key to writing. Every script I've ever written has been typed at every stage from first draft to final copy.

Since then, I have written more than eight hundred television commercials, twenty-four half-hour infomercials, two best-selling books, and one five-part ten-hour mini-series (that was never sold but was plagiarized and turned into a three-hour mini-series). I've typed hundreds of letters outlining offers that have successfully recruited more than eighty Hollywood stars to be part of my commercials and infomercials. Where would I be if I hadn't learned to type?

Even though Steven Spielberg and I did not achieve success in anything "significant" in high school, the "insignificant" things we did achieve success in became the launching pads and cornerstones of our current and future success.

Did Steven Spielberg and I have any idea how significant these seemingly insignificant things were or would become? Not a clue. In fact, I ran into Steven at a restaurant in Beverly Hills right after he received his second royalty check from *ET* (reported to be $98 million). It was the first time we had seen each other since high school. He came over to the table, and as we talked about Arcadia High, I looked up at him and said, "Steven, if only I had known . . ." And he bent down and whispered, "My God, if only *I* had known." He then told my guests that in high school he had figured he would end up as a studio musician.

What was true for Steven Spielberg and Steve Scott is equally true for you. There is no such thing as insignificant success. Anything you've ever succeeded at is important and can be a major stepping-stone to your future success.

INSIGHT 3: TAKE A CLOSE LOOK AND DISCOVER WHAT "INSIGNIFICANT" SUCCESSES YOU HAVE HAD AND FOCUS ON THEM. THEY COULD WELL BECOME THE FOUNDATION OF YOUR FUTURE ACHIEVEMENTS.

Notebook for Success

Finding Gold Where You Least Expect It

The purpose of this section is to give you a quick review of the insights and laws that I have found relevant to achieving success and to help you evaluate your strengths and weaknesses. The key to success is learning to minimize your weaknesses and maximize your strengths. You'll need to start a notebook to complete the exercises.

INSIGHTS FOR SUCCESS (REVIEW)

Insight 1: Past achievement is not a true predictor of future success.

Insight 2: If you can do one thing well—even if it doesn't seem significant—you have the potential for phenomenal success.

Insight 3: Take a close look and discover what "insignificant" successes you have had and focus on them. They could well become the foundation of your future achievements.

Laws for Achieving Success

Law of Past Failures: Don't use your past failures or lack of achievement as an excuse or limitation for your lack of achievement in the present or future. The former does not control the latter.

PERSONAL INVENTORY FOR SUCCESS

1. List areas in your past that you consider failures—for example, high school or college grades, past jobs in which you saw disappointing results (firings, failures, or mediocre performance).

2. List what you consider your greatest weaknesses, both personally and professionally—lack of education, lack of career achievement, impatience, short temper, and so forth.

3. List any area of success you have ever accomplished, significant or insignificant, in school, athletics, business, friendships, relationships, and so forth.

4. Write down the feelings you had when you achieved that success—whether it was a grade, a promotion, or a friend saying thank-you for your advice. Reach back when thinking about the feelings. They can be as recent as a few hours ago or as distant as your early childhood.

5. Make a list of the things you do really well, no matter how important or unimportant you think they are. (For me it's typing, persuading, teaching, and seeing the logical order in things. I'm also good at encouraging other people and helping them solve problems.) Make the list as long or as short as you want, but make it! These are the strengths that you are going to be building on.

6. Finally, make a list of the things you love to do. It doesn't matter if they fall under business, recreation, social activities, or any other category.

CHAPTER 2

You're Fired!

Failure . . . the Most Often Missed Key to Extraordinary Success

Fired once, fired twice, failed once, failed twice, and quit five other companies—and that was in my first six years after college.

INSIGHT 1: PAST FAILURES DON'T HAVE TO LIMIT YOUR FUTURE.

Law of Learning: Failures are the second best teachers we have. Don't despise them, learn from them.

Any personnel manager looking at my resume in 1976 would have been impressed with my "stated goals and accomplishments." But if he was worth his salt, he would have looked beneath the "veneer" and focused on the length of each employment and how each stint had ended. Here's what he would have seen:

COLLEGE CLASS OF 1970

Year	Job Number	Salary	Duration/Outcome
1971	1	$600/month	4 months/Quit
	2	Started business	8 months/Failed
1972	3	$1,000/month	9 months/Fired
1973	4	$1,000/month	9 months/Quit
1974	5	$1,100/month	5 months/Quit
1974	6	Started business	9 months/Failed
1975	7	$1,000/month	4 months/Fired
1975	8	$1,100/month	4 months/Quit
1976	9	$1,500/month	4 months/Quit

Even if nothing else in this book can make you believe that anyone can succeed, the above resume should be all the proof you need. Although I could write a whole chapter about each of my first nine jobs, I'll touch on only a few relevant points. You'll see that I am not different from you. In fact, most of you are probably at least a little ahead of where I was.

In 1970 I was graduated from Arizona State University with a degree in marketing. Once again I didn't graduate top in my class or even top in my field. I was a "B" student who rarely studied and always crammed. Out of the forty courses I took in college, only a handful—certainly no more than seven—made any contribution to me personally or professionally. What I did have, however, was two or three wonderful professors who motivated me to learn how to sell and how to market. Even though I didn't get too many A's in their classes, they perceived my enthusiasm and consequently wrote encouraging notes on my term papers that motivated me all the more.

When I graduated, I quickly discovered that there were no marketing jobs in Phoenix for an inexperienced would-be marketer, so my first job was in a management training program for a life insurance agency. The head of the agency was a wonderful man named Robert Grange. He was the most incredible salesman I had ever met and he was a master at the use of silence in the art of persuasion. He made two important contributions to my life and career. First, he blew me away when he told me that even though my starting salary was only $500 per month, by the time I retired I would have earned a total of $250,000 in my lifetime. That number that was so much higher than I had expected, it added a degree of self-worth to my self-esteem. Second, he taught me a selling technique, using questions and silence, that has been a big part of my success as a mass-market salesman. (I'll touch on that in another chapter.)

Anyway, I lasted only four months on that job because I wasn't much of a life insurance salesman. Ironically, though, by 1978 I had learned how to sell life insurance policies in one hundred seconds (instead of the six hours it takes the average life insurance salesman). By 1987 I had sold hundreds of thousands of policies, generating more than $100 million in premiums. So, all things considered, in the end I guess I could sell life insurance.

I quit my job with Mr. Grange to start a business with three friends—two businessmen who were going to put up the money, and one of my best friends, who along with me was going to be a working partner. I borrowed $3,200, which I figured would last me six months because I was not receiving any salary from the financial partners. We called the business Klass Notes.

We bought three sets of notes for each of about one hundred university courses from "A" students. We edited them into one perfect set of notes for each course and then printed them. Beginning with the first day of the new semester, we handed out flyers advertising our notes as students filed out of their classrooms. Our notes were every student's dream come true.

Within one week of passing out the flyers, 85 percent of the class enrollment for the course notes we offered had purchased our notes. We were on our way to making a fortune, or so we thought. We decided we wanted to take the company national, and I met with an investor on the East Coast. He offered to put up $250,000 if we could accomplish at the University of Maryland what we had accomplished at Arizona State. My working partner, Tom Delnoce, and I packed our bags and drove to Maryland.

Because lectures are protected by common-law copyrights, no notes could be published without the written consent of the course professors. So the first step was to sign royalty contracts with the course professors. Tom and I spent our first two weeks calling on more than one hundred Maryland professors. After two weeks we had only *one* signed contract. It seemed the Maryland professors prided themselves on not requiring their students to take notes. In fact, most of them proudly admitted, "I don't even know what I'm going to say until I say it." To them it was the new wave. In two weeks our dream was dead. We quickly came up with another idea and spent another four weeks on it, only to have it, too, fail.

Tom and his wife flew back to Arizona. They had not moved their possessions to the East, although my wife and I had. We were stuck on the East Coast. We were three thousand miles from home with no money, no savings, no income, and no job, and my wife was only four days away from delivering our first child.

With my tail between my legs I drove to Philadelphia to try to get a job with the National Liberty Corporation, a mail-order insurance group founded by an acquaintance of mine. The company decided to take a chance on me, and I was hired by the marketing division as an assistant product manager. My starting salary was $1,000 per month, which in 1971 was barely enough to take care of our needs.

It was on this job that I really began to learn some critical fundamentals of marketing. I learned how to test-market; I learned the importance of testing for "breakthroughs" as well as testing for "carburetor adjustments." A "breakthrough" is a factor, such as a celebrity endorser or a price reduction, that has the potential to increase the sales response to an ad by 100 or 200 percent. A "carburetor adjustment" is a change in a headline or a piece of text (copy) that might increase response by a smaller amount, such as 10 or 20 percent.

By watching how National Liberty tested various elements I was able to learn some phenomenal lessons in marketing—such as which elements of advertising and media campaigns worked and which did not. I gained the insights and knowledge that would be the key to launching my future success. It was here that I discovered what was to become my formula for writing successful magazine and newspaper ads—a formula that I used seven years later to "outpull" one of the leading mail-order writers of all time by five to one.

Here, too, I learned the value of the right celebrity endorser: The right one could increase your sales tenfold, while the wrong one could destroy sales. National Liberty was on the cutting edge of mail-order marketing, spending more money on media and market testing than any other advertiser in the world. I was soaking up information like a sponge. So even though they were paying me only me $1,000 a month (and never gave me a raise), the knowledge they were giving me turned out to be worth hundreds of millions of dollars.

After a few months I had mastered the mechanics of the job and wanted to become more involved in the creative elements of our department, namely, working with the ad agency in the development of the print and television advertising. I was quickly told by my boss and his boss that that was not part of my job. I was reminded that my job was to analyze the response to our ads and to analyze the profitability of each market and newspaper in which we ran our ads. I was far too low on the totem pole to be involved with the creative side of the business.

I soon grew bored and started to look for extra work I could do on the side that would be more creative. I went to the other divisions of the company and did unpaid work on the side just to develop my own creativity. A president of one of the other divisions thought I was talented and asked if I would like to work for him, creating various sales materials for his agency sales force. I said yes, and he said he would have me transferred to his division the following week.

Meanwhile, my boss heard through the grapevine that I was going to be transferred. Four days before this was to happen, he called me into his office. He told me that in his entire career, I was his biggest disappointment. Of all the people he had ever hired, I had the least talent. He told me that I couldn't even adequately handle the mechanics of the job, much less the creative elements. He then said something I'll never forget: "You'll never succeed in marketing. You're fired! Clean out your desk right now."

Even though I knew that in four days I would be starting with the division on the floor just beneath us, the shock of being fired and told that I would never succeed was too much for this twenty-four-year-old with a one-year-old daughter to handle. I broke down and cried.

As I walked back to my desk, I noticed everyone in my department sneaking glances at me. He had told the entire department what he was going to do while I was at lunch. It was the single most humiliating moment of my career. As it turned out, the impact of this humiliation didn't last long because six months later the most important event in my career took place.

I was recruited by the head of yet another division to work with him. His name was Bob Marsh. I had wanted to work for Bob from the very beginning, but his division had no openings. This was my chance to really shine for the man in the company that I respected the most. Unfortunately, in spite of all our efforts, that venture failed, and the team was disbanded. Bob told me that as much as he wanted to, he couldn't protect me from the people who wanted me out of the company. He said they were planning to fire me over his objections. So I quit, moved back to Arizona, and went to work for the state's largest savings and loan.

You're probably wondering why the project that failed was so important to my career. You'll understand why when you read Chapter 4.

In the three years that followed: I worked as the marketing research director for the savings and loan for six months; started and ran a marketing consulting company for nine months; worked for a small mail-order company for four months; worked for a large bank for four months and a large mail-order company for four months. Nine jobs in all, counting the two businesses I had started. I had been fired from two, and my two businesses had failed. All this in my first six years after college. I was definitely not an odds-on favorite for achieving success. But in all of this, I gained some insights.

INSIGHT 2: "THREE STRIKES YOU'RE OUT" APPLIES ONLY IN BASEBALL.

Law of Closed Doors: When doors slam shut, get creative and make a window.

My eighth job was a product management position in the marketing department of what was then the largest bank in Arizona. When I applied, the vice president of marketing sat me down and told me that even though he was very impressed with my past accomplishments, he was reluctant to hire me because, judging from my resume, I didn't seem to stay in one company for very long.

He said he didn't want to invest a lot of money in training me only to have me leave after a year or two. For me, even a year would have been a record! Anyway, I desperately needed the job because I had been out of work for six weeks, and my friends were now leaving groceries on our doorstep every week. I assured him that I was ready to get established and settle into a lifetime career. Even though the situation didn't work out that way, I meant what I said at the time. He hired me two weeks later, but in a typically corporate foolish sort of way.

The authorized salary range for the job I was applying for was $13,000 to $16,500. He had asked me what my minimum requirements were, and I told him $13,400. (When I said minimum, I really *meant* minimum.) He could have been a real hero by offering me $15,000 or $16,000; instead, the day I received the call saying I had been hired, I was told my starting salary would be $13,200. Why would anybody be so penny wise and pound foolish?

What kind of vice president gets a thrill out of saving $200 on someone's annual salary? He thought he was cutting a good deal for the bank, saving them $200. In reality he was not only cutting a horrible deal for the bank but he was cutting a horrible deal for his department. Had he won my heart and mind, I honestly believe I would have come up with programs that would have made the bank millions of dollars and made him a superhero. But instead of thinking, "How can I make this kid so excited he'll work night and day to make us a fortune?" he thought, "How cheap can I get him?" A loyal, creative, persistent, diligent mind over the span of a career is minimally worth hundreds of thousands of dollars, and more likely millions—in my case, hundreds of millions. And yet his vision of its worth was "minus $200."

He won the battle because I couldn't afford to go without work another day, but he lost the war. I gave the bank a good four months, creating a program that paid for my salary several times over, but when another company offered me $18,000, they won my heart, my mind, and, ultimately, a campaign that doubled their annual sales—from $30 million to $60 million in a single year. Which view of employee potential and hiring do you think pays the biggest dividends?

Corporate VPs, *wake up!* When you treat your people right—even in the hiring stage—the payback will be a hundredfold, a thousandfold, or even a millionfold! Most people use only 8 percent of their brain. Motivate them to want to use 10 percent, and your department will become the "star of the company."

The insight for this section is "'Three strikes you're out' applies only in baseball." There are many ways we give up much too early in a career. We get three strikes against us, and psychologically we go back to the dugout. It's not that we quit a job or sit at home and collect unemployment, it's that we stop being creative and innovative. We stop dreaming. We stop trying to learn and grow. We just settle in and do only what is expected, and no more. We simply mark time between weekends.

After eight jobs in five years and progressing only from $1,000 a month to $1,100 a month in four years, it would have been easy to give up in a dozen different ways. The worst kind of surrender would have been a surrender in attitude, to think, "This is as good as it's going to get, so I might as well accept that this is the best I can do." But no matter what my bosses said about me, no matter what my history with jobs and salary said about me, I never stopped trying to think of better ways to sell and market whatever goods or services my employer was offering. And I never stopped dreaming about different businesses I could someday develop.

INSIGHT 3: WORK TO MEET YOUR NEEDS, BUT DREAM TO GET AHEAD.

Law of Dream Conversion: Convert dreams into goals, goals into tasks, and tasks into steps.

During those first six years, I was struggling just to survive. Two failed businesses left me seriously in debt. Each of my jobs paid barely enough to cover current expenses. Nothing was left over at the end of each month to lower my debt or put into savings. But even though I had no reason to be optimistic, I never got depressed. More important, I never resigned myself to accepting failure or mediocrity.

While I gave each of my employers my mind and body from nine to five, I saved "after hours" for dreaming. This plan is not a good idea if you're happy with your job and want to advance within your company. Most companies today expect a lot more from their employees. Had any of my employers shown any appreciation for my opinion and creativity, they would have owned my mind for twelve hours a day instead of only eight. But they wanted to mold me into a person who provides a mechanical service, simply "satisfying" a job description. So I gave them what they wanted and saved the best for after work hours.

Finally, in my ninth job (at Ambassador Leather), my boss did give me the chance to be creative. In three months I created a marketing campaign—along with Bob Marsh, the man you'll read about in Chapter 4—that doubled their annual sales from $30 million to $60 million. I quit the month after Bob and I had created that campaign so that Bob and I could start a brand-new business together.

When I handed my letter of resignation to Mike Siegal, the company's CEO, he offered to double my salary, from $18,000 to $36,000, and make me vice president of marketing. It was 1976, and I was twenty-seven. Both the salary and the position would have fulfilled my career goals, but had I accepted it, I would have traded what was to become the opportunity of a lifetime, and millions of dollars of personal income, for a mere salary and a position. What is amazing is that even though my campaign was increasing the company's sales by $30 million, the raise he offered was only $18,000. It was a lot, in relation to what I had been making, but it was *nothing* in relation to what I had just made for the company. This thinking is typical of large corporations today. Of course, it is not realistic to think that you can give every employee a significant piece of the money he has generated for the company, but when someone hits a grand slam out of the stadium and beyond the parking lot, you need to give him more than a pat on the back.

Anyway, I told Mike I was moving to Philadelphia to start a new business with the person who had engineered the campaign we had just created. I told him it was my one shot to hit a home run. He said, "Steve, these things never work out. Why give up a great job with a solid company?" I was leaving a booming catalogue company for a dream that he said most likely would turn into a nightmare.

Law of Least Resistance: The path of least resistance rarely leads to success.

It would have been easy to listen to Mike, but I just couldn't. Even if this dream didn't have a pot of gold in store, I felt that just being in business with the other dreamer who offered me the job would be fulfilling in itself. I was right. Had we never made a fortune, being in business with Bob Marsh and my other partners day in and day out for twenty years is in itself one of the most wonderful experiences of my life.

Today the company I left is out of business, and our "dream" has become the most productive company in the United States. So remember that if you are in a job which doesn't allow you to dream and be creative and innovative, don't stop dreaming. Set aside a little time each week to dream and think of ways to use your interests, loves, and talents in the future.

Notebook for Success

Dreaming—The First Step Toward Success

INSIGHTS FOR SUCCESS (REVIEW)

Insight 1: Past failures don't have to limit your future.
Insight 2: "Three strikes you're out" applies only in baseball.
Insight 3: *Work* to meet your needs but *dream* to get ahead.

Laws for Achieving Success

Law of Learning: Failures are the second best teachers we have. Don't despise them, learn from them.
Law of Closed Doors: When doors slam shut, get creative and make a window.
Law of Dream Conversion: Convert dreams into goals, goals into tasks, and tasks into steps.
Law of Least Resistance: The path of least resistance rarely leads to success.

PERSONAL INVENTORY FOR SUCCESS

1. Look at the list of "failures" you wrote down in this section of Chapter 1 and write down any general or specific lessons you learned from each failure.
2. Look at your job, your relationships, your projects, and see if you are repeating any of the mistakes that led to your past failures. Did you learn your lessons, or are you making the same mistakes again?
3. If you are making the same types of mistakes, write down the specific things you can do to correct those mistakes in your current personal and business relationships and projects.
4. Write a list of "general" dreams you wish you could

make happen. You can't make your dreams come true in your relationships, job, and career unless you have a clear picture of what those dreams are.

5. Take each dream on the list and write as detailed and specific a description of that dream as possible.

6. For each dream, create a goal using as few words as possible, preferably a single sentence.

7. Arrange your goals according to priority. For example, mine are:

- Have as personal and intimate a relationship with God as I can.
- Be the best husband I can be.
- Be the best father I can be.
- Increase my company's sales to $400 million per year by 1997.
- Make a positive impact on friends.
- Make a positive impact on others.

8. For each goal, starting with your number one priority, make a list of the general tasks necessary to achieve it. Here's my general task list for my second goal:

Goal: *Be the best husband I can be.*

- Ask my wife to tell me each area of our relationship in which she thinks I can improve. Take notes.
- Ask my wife for advice on specific things I can do or stop doing to improve in each of those areas.
- Make a list of what I can do to improve.
- Begin to make an effort to do those things as often as I can.
- Ask my wife for all the help she can give me to improve in those areas that need improvement.
- Watch the Gary Smalley video series "Hidden Keys to Loving Relationships" with pen and notepad in hand.

9. Take each of the general tasks, and if the specific action

called for isn't crystal clear, write as specific and detailed a list of "steps" as you can. Assign a target date or time to accomplish each step.

10. Actually take each step you've listed, but just like walking, take only one step at a time. Like the Nike ads say, "Just do it."

CHAPTER 3

"You'll Never Succeed" and Other Observations of My Former Corporate Bosses

When to Listen and When to Ignore the Advice and Assessments of Others

Criticism can be our friend or enemy, depending on its motive, its accuracy, and our response.

INSIGHT 1: DON'T LET SMALL MINDS LIMIT YOUR THINKING.

In 1972, I was twenty-four years old and working for the National Liberty Corporation, the first major national corporation I was employed by. As an inexperienced kid I was easily impressed by the lavish corporate headquarters, the pin-striped suits running around, and the impressive credentials of the corporate officers. There were MBAs out the kazoo, and many of the officers in our division had formerly been shining stars of other Fortune 500 companies.

Every time any of these highly experienced, highly degreed executives spoke, I listened with awe, thinking they must all be geniuses. They told me what I was supposed to do and how I was supposed to do it. I listened and I did my best to do what they said. In the beginning, I even did a lot of things that weren't included in my job description. But every time I approached my boss, his boss, or the ultimate boss with an idea, I was quickly reminded that my job was not to be creative—*that* was the job of the ad agency and the senior marketing officers.

The problem was, they were neither as smart as *they* thought they were nor as smart as *I* thought they were. In many cases the real motivation was not the advancement of the company but rather personal advancement. So when I naively took them an idea, it was doomed—not because it was bad, but because it wasn't *their* idea and, in their opinion, I was too young and inexperienced to have a profound idea.

INSIGHT 2: "YOUNG AND INEXPERIENCED" IS NOT A VALID REASON TO IGNORE OR STIFLE CREATIVE IDEAS AND ACTIVITIES.

For years most of my employers ignored my ideas and discouraged my creative activities with that excuse. Unfortunately, my employers were no different from most companies today. As a result, they discourage, frustrate, and often defeat their younger employees. At the same time, they shortchange their company shareholders because that "would-be" Babe Ruth never steps up to the plate and takes a swing. Imagine how different pro sports would be if younger players were not allowed to make the starting rosters until they were in their early to mid-forties.

"Don't be ridiculous," you say. "That's true only in sports because they rely on the physical prowess of youth. You can't compare sports to business because business relies on a person's mental and emotional abilities, which must adequately mature to make capable managerial decisions." My response to that is yes and no. Yes, we need maturity and experience to give overall guidance and direction to a business. And sports is no different. You would not recruit a new college graduate to coach a major league team. You need a seasoned professional who can make judgment calls in the middle of chaos and crisis, without panicking or overreacting to the moment. But while it's the seasoned coaches who create the game plan, it's the "kids" who hit the home runs, throw the double plays, and pitch the shutouts.

If you're a manager in business, you need to see yourself as a coach first and a player second, giving guidance, direction, and encouragement to those beneath you. Don't use the excuse that those underneath you are "too young and inexperienced" to keep them from coming up to the plate and swinging the bat. The more swings they take, the more pitches they'll hit; and the more they hit, the more runs you'll score. And don't be surprised if from among the rookies a Mickey Mantle or Ted Williams rises to the surface.

Had the executives at Universal Studios used youth and inexperience as criteria for assignments, they would never have trusted a young and inexperienced director (he was twenty-seven and had never directed a feature film) to direct the adapted screenplay of a best-selling novel. But they didn't focus on his youth or inexperience, and Steven Spielberg ended up directing his first feature film, which gave the studio their first $200 million blockbuster: *Jaws*.

For years Hollywood has been giving youth and inexperience a chance, and for years they have reaped the rewards. But you say, "That's Hollywood, not business." I could fill a Business Hall of Fame with the names of rookies who have hit business grand-slam home runs, but usually they had to hit them outside of the major corporations. We have personal computers and word processing programs thanks to rookies who most likely were never hired by a major corporation, and if they had been, they would never have made it to middle management. Their ideas would have been rejected instantly with memos listing all the mature and logical reasons that their ideas didn't have a snowball's chance of succeeding.

But fortunately for all of us, Steven Jobs and Bill Gates were too young and inexperienced to realize that the world didn't need personal computers and word processing software. In their youth and naïveté they gave us all a way to do our jobs a thousand times more efficiently and effectively. Steve and Bill, thank you, thank you! If it weren't for you two rookies, only one out of every ten scripts I've created would have been written. My sales, my success, my partners, and my employees have all prospered because you guys stepped up to the plate and took a swing when you were young. I'm glad you're both rich above suspicion. You deserve every penny!

Law of Realism: Be realistic but not conventional.

When I was twenty-seven, my ninth employer, Ambassador Leather, headed by Mike Siegal, did give me the chance to step up to the plate in the bottom of the ninth with bases loaded and two men out. My immediate supervisor (marketing manager) and his boss (vice president of marketing) both jealously guarded their positions, and when I was given the chance to bat by Mike, they were sitting on the bench—sure (and hoping) that I would strike out.

Even though Mike scared me with the news that if I struck out, I was going to be sweeping the dugout, he was still a good enough coach to send me to the plate. Thanks, Mike. I will always be grateful. When I hit the grand slam, it was really my coach (who deserved the credit for putting me in) and my batting coach (Bob Marsh) who had told me when and where and how to swing that caused that ball to go out of the park. Our home run nearly doubled Ambassador's sales—from $30 million to about $60 million—in a single year.

The first insight for this chapter is "Don't let small minds limit your thinking." Those small minds could be in brilliant, capable people, but they might be small in their thinking about you, your abilities, and your potential contributions. The vice president at National Liberty who fired me was extremely capable and in fact ultimately rose to the company's presidency. There was no smallness of mind in his dealings with corporate strategies and tactics, but his attitude toward me and my immediate supervisor was extremely small.

He was not only quick to belittle and discard any marketing or creative ideas I had, he was quick to remind my boss and me that he was the brain and we were simply the "mechanics" of the department. With a simple smirk he could make you feel like an idiot for even suggesting an idea. His "smallness" was further demonstrated by his constant criticism, and it was shown the humiliating way he fired me in front of our department four days before I was to be transferred.

All of this is to say that you should not believe those who think small about you, no matter how smart and experienced they may appear. Listen to everything they say. Capitalize on their wisdom and experience. But when they try to belittle you, your ideas, or your abilities, listen politely but in your mind tell them they don't know what they are talking about. The only person who has the right to limit your thinking and your abilities is you, and even you shouldn't do it!

INSIGHT 3: YOU MAY BE A LOT SMARTER THAN YOUR BOSSES.

Law of Strengths: Play to your strengths.
Law of Weaknesses: Strengthen your weaknesses.

The day my boss at National Liberty fired me, I'm sure he thought that was the last time he would ever have to deal with me. *Wrong, wrong, wrong.* Five years later he had the humiliating experience of being forced to stick his head into my office at a completely different company and thank me for creating the most profitable marketing project in his division.

You see, after Bob Marsh and I had been in business for a year, successfully selling products on TV, Bob had the idea that we could sell life insurance the same way. He took the idea to the owner of National Liberty Corporation. The company had tried to use TV to sell life insurance in the past but had failed miserably and had given up on the idea years earlier. At first they resisted the idea completely, but Bob made them an offer he thought they couldn't refuse. Our little company would not only hire the spokesman and produce the commercials, we would pay for it—unlike any media company or ad agency in America. In other words, we'd put our money where our mouth was and bear all the financial risk.

Here's where the story becomes an eye-opener. Bob said we were willing to take this risk on one condition: If the test was successful, instead of paying our company a standard "media commission," National Liberty would buy the leads we generated at a fair price, a price *less* than what they were currently spending to generate leads from other media—a price that would be incredibly profitable for them.

Think about it: We were willing to take all the risk, and in return, if the program worked, they would make *more* profit per policy than they were currently making. They were in a can't-lose position. If the program didn't work, our company would lose all the money. They would lose none! If the program did work, we would make money, and they would make more money per policy than they were currently making any other way!

Is that a "no-brainer" or what? Still, my ex-boss and his fellow vice presidents didn't want to give us the go-ahead. Why? Because if the program was super-successful, Bob and I could end up making more money personally than my ex-boss and the other vice presidents of the company. And—horror of horrors—Bob and I were ex-employees! They couldn't handle the thought of ex-employees making more money than they were making. It didn't matter to them that the insurance company itself would make a lot more money for their shareholders than our company would make.

Bob was furious, and met with the founder and owner of the company, Arthur DeMoss. Art couldn't believe that the proposition had been turned down by his subordinates, but he didn't feel good about overruling them outright. With that, Bob made an offer the company really couldn't refuse. He said: Let your current ad agencies produce a commercial with your current spokesperson, and we'll test it against ours. If their commercial gets a better response than ours, we'll work on the standard commission basis. But if ours beats theirs, you buy the leads at the agreed-upon price, which will still make your company more money than any other project or campaign you have.

With that offer, the small minds agreed, thinking there was no way that our little company could beat their giant ad agency. To stack the deck against us further, they made us agree they could see our script before shooting theirs, so if it had points that they liked better than the ones submitted by their agency, they could incorporate them into their agency scripts. We agreed, and the game was on.

After receiving our scripts, they did give a lot of our ideas to their ad agency. Their agency produced super-slick commercials with their "celebrity endorser" who gave an equally slick performance on camera.

I shot our commercial with Senator Sam Ervin, who was eighty years old at the time (six years after his famed Watergate hearings). Senator Ervin was a wonderful man to work with, but unlike *their* spokesman's performance, his was far from slick in front of the camera. He hobbled around from in back of a desk to the front. His speech was slow and somewhat disjointed, but it was 100 percent classic Sam Ervin, and I was thrilled with the finished spot.

The week before the two commercials were to be broadcast in test markets, Bob Marsh was invited to National Liberty's boardroom where my former boss and the top executives of NLC were to be shown both spots. The first spot was shown featuring their slick spokesperson. When it finished, there was plenty of applause and praise. Then our spot was shown. No applause, no praise, only laughter and ridicule. One executive asked, "Why even test the Ervin spot? It's obvious the other one is going to win. It's so much better!" Everyone agreed except Bob. He immediately said that our Ervin spot would outpull the other spot by at least two to one, and he would gladly bet anyone at the table any amount of money. There was silence.

The next week we tested the spot, and the Ervin spot outpulled the other spot, not by two to one but four to one. Had the other spot been "rolled out" by NLC, they would have lost a fortune. The Ervin spot *made* them a fortune! It also made Bob, me, and our other partners (by now there were six of us) a fortune. My ex-boss's worst nightmare had come true: His former employees had given his company its most profitable program—more profitable than all of the programs developed by him and the three hundred people who worked for him— and we were personally making a lot more money from the campaign than he or any other company officer.

One day he came to our offices to have lunch with Bob. After lunch they returned to Bob's office for a brief meeting, and at the end of it Bob said, "On your way out it would be nice if you stuck your head into Steve's office and said thank-you." My ex-boss asked, "For what?" Bob said, "Isn't the Ervin campaign the most profitable campaign you've got?" "Yes," he replied. "Then I want you to thank the man who created that campaign." When my ex-boss hesitated, Bob said, "Look, Steve Scott means a lot more to me than your company's account, so if you want to see our relationship continue, you'd better say thank-you to Steve on your way out."

A few minutes later he stuck his head in my door and nearly choked on the words as they came out of his mouth: "Steve . . . I just wanted to say thanks for the Ervin campaign." I said "You're welcome" and congratulated him on his recent promotion as the company's president. There were a million things I would liked to have said, but his stopping by my office and making the comment caught me so off guard, I couldn't come up with an appropriate remark fast enough.

To date this man who fired me in such a humiliating way and told me I would never be a success in marketing has yet to build a hundred-million-dollar business while we have built many. All have been considered marketing phenomenons. My partners and I also hold every television direct-response marketing record on the books—from sales to profits to numbers of respondents. Thank God I chose not to believe my ex-boss on that humiliating day in 1972 when he fired me.

Since the insight for this section is "You may be a lot smarter than your bosses," I should end the section by saying that bosses often become bosses because they are smart in some or many areas. And even though you may be smarter than your bosses in some areas, they may be smarter than you in others. So use wisdom and gain everything you can from them, but don't let them shape your conception of your self-worth or potential.

In spite of the problems I had with my bosses at NLC, it was without doubt the most important foundational education I ever received in regard to my career. And if you're ever fortunate enough to have bosses like my partners Bob Marsh and

John Marsh, the amount you can learn is colossal! The difference is that Bob and John are not only the smartest bosses I've ever had, they're the best *coaches* I've ever had. And they are coaches first and bosses second. A good coach is a great motivator, encourager, teacher, and cheerleader. And that's what all of us should be to those around us and under our authority.

Notebook for Success

Overcoming the Number One Factor That Limits Your Success

INSIGHTS FOR SUCCESS (REVIEW)

Insight 1: Don't let small minds limit your thinking.
Insight 2: "Young and inexperienced" is not a valid reason to ignore or stifle creative ideas and activities.
Insight 3: You may be a lot smarter than your bosses.

Laws for Achieving Success

Law of Realism: Be realistic, but not conventional.
Law of Strengths: Play to your strengths.
Law of Weaknesses: Strengthen your weaknesses.

PERSONAL INVENTORY FOR SUCCESS

The purpose of this exercise is to show you how easy it is to break through the negative boundaries imposed by other people's thinking. At the same time, this exercise will help you distinguish between mere conventional thinking and realities of the situation. You don't want to be limited by conventional thinking, and yet you must face reality, respect it, and learn to use it to inspire creative alternatives.

1. List any or all recent projects or things you want to do or achieve at home or at work that are affected or thwarted by the negative comments, actions, or input of someone else.
2. Answer the following questions about the project or thing you listed above that was the most important to you or for which you had the most hope or enthusiasm.
   A. What percentage of the negative input received was based on:

    a. emotion

    b. past experience(s) or failures (theirs, yours, or others)

    c. lack of understanding or fully comprehending your goal, intention, or vision

    d. conventional thinking

    e. logic

    f. realities of the situation

  B. Was the negative input based largely on e and f? If so, you should give it a lot more weight than if it was based on a through d. Reasons a through d are fairly easy roadblocks to overcome or go around once you know how.

  C. On the other hand, if the negative input based primarily on e and f, then you should begin by reexamining your goal, project, or plan. Input based on these two criteria does not necessarily mean the death of your plan or project but may be the springboard to a creative alternative that results in an even better and more doable *revised* plan or project.

3. Review the list of your strengths or things you do really well (compiled from Chapter 1). Write down how you are using those strengths to accomplish your goals. If you are not using them to their fullest, write down how you can begin using them more effectively to achieve each goal.

4. (Optional.) Review the list of your weaknesses (compiled from Chapter 1). Make a list of the ways you think you can strengthen these areas. If you're at a loss, find someone who is strong in that area and seek his or her advice on what you can do to improve. Start with what you consider your greatest weakness. Work on only one weakness at a time.

CHAPTER 4

A Man Named Bob

Everyone Needs a Mentor . . . Here's How to Get the Right One

If everyone had this Bob for a mentor, we'd all be millionaires.

INSIGHT I: A PERSON WHO BELIEVES IN YOU IS A TREMENDOUS SOURCE OF POWER.

The rise of American Telecast is quite an amazing tale for two reasons: First, it's a story of divine guidance and intervention, and second, it's the story of a man named Bob. I first met Bob Marsh in 1971 when we both worked for the National Liberty Corporation. Bob was a corporate vice president and was a marketing and entrepreneurial genius. During my twenty-two months of working with the various divisions of this company, I had a chance to do side projects for Bob and grew to have a tremendous respect and admiration for him.

Unlike the other corporate officers who had MBAs and managerial experience with various Fortune 500 companies, Bob was simply an entrepreneur. He couldn't recite theories or create massive marketing plans or flowcharts, and in fact would never have wasted a minute of his time doing so. Instead, he was like a world champion bloodhound and could sniff out every opportunity to increase sales and profits and to cut unnecessary, wasteful spending.

In the spring of 1973, Bob recruited me along with a small team to work on a new venture at National Liberty. We worked on that project for six months, but unfortunately it failed miserably. But as I mentioned in Chapter 2, even though the project failed, it was the most important event in my career, for during that time Bob and I really got to know each other.

As we worked together, I realized that I would rather work for him than any other person on the planet. But because the project bombed and because of my past failures with the company, even Bob with all his influence couldn't protect me from those who wanted to fire me. Consequently, I quit before they could fire me. We had both gained a genuine love and respect for each other, but had no idea that four years later the entire course of our lives would change because of our relationship.

After leaving Philadelphia and moving back to Arizona, I basically lost touch with Bob until two years later. In November 1975 I was in the third month of my new job with the largest bank in Arizona. We were only one year away from the presidential election and I could tell that Gerald Ford was going to have a hard time getting reelected. As I thought about it, I realized that a media formula that Bob Marsh had created and perfected could be the key to Ford's reelection. This particular package had never been used in politics but had been incredibly successful in business.

I found out that two months earlier Bob had left the National Liberty Corporation and had purchased a small media-buying agency. I called him at his office in Philadelphia, told him my idea, and asked if he would help me make a presenta-tion to Ford's reelection committee if I could get us a meeting. He said that he thought it was a great idea to apply this partic-ular media package to politics and would be glad to pay for my airline ticket to make the presentation if I got an appointment with the top Ford people.

Within a couple of days I had one. Bob and I met in Wash-ington and made the presentation. Unfortunately for Gerald Ford, the bureaucrats surrounding him were not interested in our package. I have absolutely no doubt that had they used it, it would have given Ford the edge he needed. After the presenta-tion, we returned to Bob's home in Philadelphia.

On the train ride back from Washington, Bob asked me how I liked my job at the bank. I told him that it was okay, but com-pared to mail-order marketing, it was like going back to the dark ages.

Then I asked him if I could go to work for him. He told me that the only job he had available was for a media buyer, and I would be bored to tears doing that. I told him I didn't care, I wanted to work for him anyway. He reminded me that my tal-ents were in marketing and his company was only in the time-buying business. I was deeply disappointed.

He then asked if I had tried to get a job with any of the mail-order companies in Arizona. I replied that there was only one big one, Ambassador Leather, and they weren't hiring. He told me that he knew they were looking for a good marketing man, and he was sure that if I called the company's president and said the right things, he would hire me on the spot. I asked Bob what the right things were, and he wrote them on a piece of paper and handed it to me. As soon as I got back to Arizona, I called the president of Ambassador from my desk at the bank and went through the pitch that Bob had written for me. He was very impressed and asked if I could come in that evening for an interview. I raced to Ambassador and went through an interview with the president and three of his vice presidents. He told me that he was very interested and would call me the next day.

The next day he offered me the job with an increase of 40 percent over my current salary at the bank. I quickly gave notice and went to work for Ambassador the first week of January 1976. Once I was at Ambassador, I began working on a way to move them effectively into an aggressive newspaper insert campaign, my specialty. In the meantime, I discovered that Ambassador had a two-minute TV commercial featuring a handbag called the Everything Bag. Ambassador had a small media group in New York buying time for them and controlling the entire campaign. Even though they had had this commercial for more than a year, they had achieved only a little more than a million dollars in sales.

I called Bob and told him that I thought there was something we could do with this particular commercial to turn it into a major campaign if he could get Ambassador as an account. He asked if I could get him a meeting with the president, and I told him I would try.

The next day I told Mike Siegal, the company president, about Bob. Mike wasn't interested. But Bob said he was going to the West Coast and would come in and see me, and *maybe* I could get him a meeting with Mike anyway. I agreed to try. A week later Bob came through Phoenix with an idea that he felt could win the account. He came to the office, and I convinced Mike to meet with him for just a few minutes. It turned out that Bob was not only the most incredible marketing man I had ever met, he was also by far the best salesman. In an hour he had worked the impossible. He had convinced Mike to allow him to run a test campaign. After the meeting we gave each other a high five because we felt that this could be a very good thing for Bob's media company and for my career at Ambassador.

Two weeks later I flew to Omaha, Nebraska, to meet with the 800 service that would be taking the calls for the test campaign. Someone at the hotel happened to mention that Pat Boone was in town that weekend and was staying at the hotel. I had never met Pat but knew a man who was in business with him, so I wrote a note that said, "You don't know me, but I'm a friend of Irvin Kesler's. Your book has meant a lot to my life, and when you get in from your concert, if you would like a little fellowship, please feel free to give me a call. I won't be going to sleep until around 2:00 A.M. P.S. Please tell Irving that Steve Scott says hi."

By 11:30 P.M. I was too tired to wait up, so I went to sleep. But shortly after midnight the phone rang. "Steve? . . . Pat Boone" said the voice on the other end. The next thing I knew, we were talking about his relationship with Irving and some problems that had developed. I found myself giving Pat some business advice, and the conversation continued for nearly two and a half hours. When we hung up, we were friends. The next morning we had breakfast together, and he was every bit as nice as you would imagine.

A week later we were ready to test the campaign idea that Bob had developed for Ambassador and again flew to Omaha to watch the response at the answering service. To our delight it was a great success. When we started punching our calculators, we figured out that we could sell nearly $30 million worth of handbags by running that one commercial in a particular media campaign. We saw that Ambassador sales were going to *double* in a single year.

That night Bob and I flew from Omaha to Chicago and stayed in a friend's penthouse apartment. As we ate dinner high above the city, Bob made a comment that would change both of our lives: "If you found a product *we* could market, we could go into business together and probably make a lot more money selling products than we'll ever make selling TV time." That was the most exciting idea anyone had ever voiced to me in a single sentence. It got my juices flowing. After dinner Bob said, "Wouldn't it be amazing if someday we could build a business and afford a place like this?" Wow! A mental picture I would never forget . . . a dream that would come true many times over!

As soon as I returned to Arizona, I called Pat Boone, whom I had known at that point for all of two weeks. I told him that I had the chance to go into business with the smartest man in the world, and if he could find a product that we could market, we would create a commercial and Pat could be the spokesperson. A week later Pat gave me a call. He told me that he had found an acne medication, and he sent Bob and me some samples. After we became convinced that the product was a good one, we decided to go for it.

I gave my letter of resignation to the president of Ambassador and two weeks later moved back to Philadelphia. My first day of work with Bob Marsh was May 10, 1976. He gave me an office and a salary of $10,000 a year, which when added to a fee Ambassador had agreed to pay me to remain a consultant for a year ($18,000) gave me my first real financial windfall: a salary of $28,000 a year. Far more important than the salary, Bob gave me a significant piece of the ownership of the new marketing company that we formed, a company that ultimately became known as American Telecast Corporation, or ATC.

My responsibilities to begin with were several. Along with Bob and his son-in-law, I would help manage the Ambassador campaign, which created media sales that were very important to the company's cash flow. Second, and more important, I would write and produce a television commercial with Pat Boone and various members of his family selling our first product, an acne medication.

In early June I wrote my first commercial. I went over to Bob's house to show him what I had written. He read it and said, "It's good, but it needs a hook in the opening." I asked him what he meant by a "hook," and he told me that the commercial didn't have anything that instantly grabbed viewers and made them focus on what was about to be said.

As I thought about it, I recalled that when I was in high school I had horrible acne and had to go to the dermatologist once a week. Those weekly visits were physical torture. Not only did I have my face burned with ultraviolet rays, but the doctor lanced all the bad pimples and poked at my face for fifteen to twenty minutes, until it was throbbing with pain. I also thought about how embarrassed I was by my pockmarked complexion.

Thinking about all that, the perfect *hook* came to mind: *"Acne is painful, both physically and emotionally. I don't care if you're a teenager or an adult, acne causes embarrassment and anxiety."* I had created my first hook.

With script in hand, I flew to Hollywood and directed my first commercial. I had a budget of $3,600 and was sick when all the bills came in and I found out I had spent $4,200. The cash flow in our company was very poor at the time, and this was nearly all the money that Bob had set aside for the project. Yet, rather than criticize me for going over budget, he reassured me and said that somehow we'd make it through the test.

The day before the test, he came into my office and said something I'll never forget. He said that if the test bombed and he had to let everyone else go, as long as he had a dollar in his pocket, we'd be partners—even if it meant starting all over. Needless to say, the tears began to flow. To hear this kind of commitment at the age of twenty-seven from someone I loved and admired was overwhelming.

The day came to run our two-minute test commercial. Our whole future was riding on it. It was airing on WXON in Detroit at 4:58 P.M. We knew that we needed fifteen orders to have any hope for a business. We also knew that the handbag commercial for Ambassador routinely generated about twenty-five orders on this spot. So if we got twenty-five orders, we'd have a big winner capable of making millions of dollars.

After waiting on pins and needles all day, the hour was finally at hand. The commercial ran from 4:58 to 5:00. At 5:00 we began dialing the 800 number. Busy! We dialed again. Busy again. And again and again and again. For five minutes, nothing but busy signals! We were generating enough calls to tie up all the lines at this small answering service. At 5:05 I finally got through and asked the owner how many orders he had taken. "How many do you want?" was his reply. "Come on, Jerry. Just tell me how many we got." And then came the answer that changed my world. "Would you be happy with fifty-two in the first five minutes?"

I burst into tears and started whooping. "How many? How many?" Bob asked. When I told him fifty-two, everyone in the office heard our shouts. It was only one airing on one station, and yet it was double the response of the handbag. We knew we had a giant winner. In the next year that little $4,200 commercial generated $20 million in sales.

INSIGHT 2: DON'T BE GREEDY. SHARE THE WEALTH, DON'T HOARD IT.

Law of Motivation: Expressed appreciation and more money are great motivators.
Law of Relationships: Strive to create "win-win" relationships and deals.

One of Bob's lifetime goals was to create a business that he could one day share with his two sons and his two sons-in-law. The success of that first project made it possible to bring them into the business within the first year. They started as salaried employees, but as the business grew, each one began to assume more and more responsibility. By the end of the second year each one was running a critical area of the business, and Bob had given them each a piece of the company.

All of us would have been thrilled just to work for Bob and earn a salary, but Bob was not only wonderfully generous, he was wonderfully smart. He believed that by giving each of us a significant part of the business he would accomplish two goals. First, we would all be highly motivated to do whatever it took to increase the business. Second, we would all be supportive of one another because if one of us succeeded, we all succeeded, and if one of us failed, we all failed. He also knew from experience that there is no greater incentive to succeed than owning a business.

Bob's philosophy of sharing the winnings with the horses who run the race didn't stop with the five of us. It set off a chain reaction that proved to be one of the most powerful expansionary forces in our business. The idea of giving a piece of the profits to people who brought us products and ideas resulted in a lot of great products finding their way to our company while they were in the developmental stage.

Bob was once told by a financier that true success was not measured by the number of millions you make but by the number of million*aires* you make. By that measure Bob and our company are incredibly successful. Not only have all the partners made millions but also people who have connected us with various inventors and authors have made millions in finder's fees; authors and inventors have made millions in license fees; and countless celebrities have made millions in royalties. In all, more than forty people have become millionaires or made over a million dollars through our efforts. Apart from the celebrities, not one of the finders, authors, or inventors had any serious money prior to meeting American Telecast.

For example, one housewife introduced us to a college professor who had an educational seminar. She became a millionaire, and he became a multimillionaire. And that's more the norm than the exception. It's a philosophy that took our company from zero in product sales in 1975 to over $150 million in 1992 and over $230 million in 1994.

Many observers have told us that we pay our celebrities a lot more than they're worth. And yet we know that the right celebrity on the right product increases the sales of the product beyond its potential. On top of that, we want these celebrities to make millions because it makes it easier to recruit others to the new projects we create. But as you'll see in Chapter 9, getting the right celebrity for the right product isn't just a matter of money and is a lot more difficult than one would think. That's why celebrity endorsers are often disasters for some of our competitors, and by and large have been avoided in the advertising industry.

The skeptic will say that cutting the pie in so many pieces may result in a big sales volume but will wreak havoc on profits. Wrong! Our profits as a percentage of sales are more than double that of the nation's top ten retailers, more than double that of any catalogue company, and more than double that of the home shopping networks.

Does the "share the wealth" principle work? When wisely used with the right people, there is no other power like it. Even though the pie gets divided into more pieces, the *size* of the pie increases geometrically! A small piece of a giant pie is a lot better than a huge piece of a miniature pie. Said another way, would you prefer to have 100 percent of a gold nugget or 10 percent of a gold mine? I hope the rest of the business world (especially our competitors) never wake up to this fact. It could make our job a lot harder.

INSIGHT 3: WHO YOU WORK FOR IS AS IMPORTANT AS WHAT YOU DO.

In my first six years after college I had a total of ten bosses. Until boss nine (Mike Siegal at Ambassador) and boss ten (Bob Marsh), my contributions to my employers were mediocre at best. When I went to work for Mike Siegal, in only three months my efforts produced a doubling of the company's annual sales, from $30 million to $60 million. When I went to work for Bob Marsh, my first four months on the job resulted in the business going from no sales to $20 million in sales our first year. Why was Steve Scott so productive under bosses nine and ten and yet so unproductive for bosses one through eight? Had I gained a level of intelligence and creativity all of a sudden? Of course not. I was the same person that I had been under all my bosses. So what was different?

The difference was the bosses! Bosses one through eight viewed me as a wet-nosed kid who was always coming up with marketing and advertising ideas that distracted me from fully focusing on the mechanics of my job. Those men made two mistakes.

First, they were so concerned about their own career paths that they feared any subordinate coming up with better ideas than they had. Even when one of my ideas was adopted, my bosses would downplay its significance to me (lest I think I should get a raise) while taking credit for the idea or the results of the idea with their bosses (so they could get the raise.)

While working for National Liberty in 1972, I made a decision to go out on a limb and place orders for more advertising than my department had been budgeted. My boss found out after the orders had been placed and lambasted me. When the ads ran, the sales and profits went through the roof. The next quarter, the business did a major downturn, and it was my overbudget expenditures that had saved the day.

Did my boss say thank-you? No! He never even admitted to me that my "mistake" had been a windfall for the company. He did go before the board of directors, however, and take credit for the "insightful added expenditures of the second quarter," stating that he had anticipated the downturn in the third quarter and had decided to raise expenditures accordingly in the second quarter to compensate for the downturn. Needless to say, he was praised by the CEO and the board, and never acknowledged that I was the person who had made the "insightful decision," only to have been castigated by him.

The second mistake my early bosses made with me was not listening to my ideas because I was only in my early twenties and didn't have the then-coveted MBA—what could I possibly know? In the previous chapter, I dealt with this problem that so many young, inexperienced people face in their early careers.

Insight 4: There is no greater motivation than love.

Law of Love: Love people. *Use* things. *Not vice versa.*

I couldn't write a chapter about Bob Marsh without revealing one of the most critical secrets to our success. Bob, like all of us, was partly driven by his desire to see his company achieve success. But anyone who knows Bob knows that his desire for success is not and was not the greatest driving force in his life. What he was really driven by, both at home and on the job, was love. Above all he wanted to see each of the partners and our employees happy and successful. That love gave him the willingness to let us develop our own areas in our own ways, and gave him incredible patience with our weaknesses and failures. His love not only motivated us to do our best in terms of our efforts, but it also motivated us to endure and work out any problems we had with one another. We knew that if we didn't get along, it would really hurt Bob, and our love for him became the cord that tied us all together.

If you're a corporate manager, you're probably thinking that such a system is good for a small business but could never work in a big company. That's not true. Love for your employees and fellow workers is not a gooey, gushy, emotional feeling. Rather, it's a day-by-day demonstration of consideration, honor, recognition, and valuing individuals for themselves. It's listening to their dumb ideas (which sometimes turn out to be brilliant); it's being quick to encourage and praise; it's learning to give gentle correction without assailing criticism. That kind of love can be incorporated into any workplace. It doesn't require a feeling, it requires a decision—a decision to honor and encourage and make *their* success and happiness an important part of your job. The more successful those beneath you become, the more successful you become. And the nice thing is, you'll not only become more successful, you'll stay happy along the way.

Law of Mentors: Be smart: find a mentor or a coach to get even smarter.

Name one great athlete who ever achieved greatness without a coach. Find one great scientist who didn't have a mentor who inspired him to greatness. Nearly every highly successful person has had at least one mentor or coach. The need for a mentor or coach does not end when we play our last little league game. There is virtually no stage in life in which we don't need a coach. This observation is especially true in business. Bob Marsh has been my mentor and coach, and everything in my life would have been radically different, and my entire career and 99.9 percent of my success would be nonexistent, if I hadn't had a mentor named Bob.

If the only benefit you obtain from this book is the motivation to find a mentor or coach, this book will have been worth its weight in gold. All of us had coaches or mentors in our early years—whether our parents, a coach, a teacher, a friend, or our first supervisor on a job. But for most of us, achieving true success requires that we have a mentor or series of mentors throughout our lives. True, some people achieve success without mentors, but it's a much harder and less rewarding road. So where and how do you find a great coach or mentor for your needs right now? The process can be as easy as asking someone you respect if you could have a little of his or her time to acquire some advice, or it can be as complex as creating a strategy for finding and approaching someone you never met. Some specific strategies and techniques are given below.

STRATEGIES AND TIPS FOR IDENTIFYING AND RECRUITING MENTORS

1. Determine the specific area of your life or profession for which you want a mentor. Do you need a mentor to help you in relationships, to help you in your profession in general, or to help you in a particular area of your job, career, or profession, such as managerial skills, marketing skills, and so forth? (I've had two important mentors in the areas of relationships and one key mentor in business.)
2. Create a list of potential mentors for each area you've decided on. Follow the order given in step number one of the Personal Inventory for Success on page 75.
3. Starting with the mentors at the top of your list and working down, write down the status of your current relationship with each one (boss, friend, acquaintance, friend of a friend, total stranger, and so forth).
4. Write down everything you know about that person

through either your personal experience with him or her, or second- or third-hand knowledge.

5. Research everything you can about your potential mentors. What are their likes, their dislikes, their passions? How do they spend their time on and off the job? What motivates them, and so forth?

6. If they're mere acquaintances or strangers to you, do you know anyone they know? If you do, begin to find out all you can from that person and consider using that person as a reference when you make your initial contact with the potential mentor.

7. Prepare to contact a potential mentor on the phone or in writing with a brief proposal or request. Whether you plan to make your contact in person, on the phone, or in a letter, you need to prepare your proposal or request well before you make the contact. If you are contacting someone who knows your reference but doesn't know you, the name of your reference should be given in your opening sentence. Your next sentence should touch on the quality or qualities that you admire about this person. You should then briefly explain why those qualities are so important to you and how you want to gain this person's insight and wisdom in making those qualities a part of your life. Finally, ask if the person can spare a little time each week or month (a lunch, a breakfast, a coffee break, a round of golf) in which you can acquire information that will help you grow in this particular area.

8. Make the contact. Nothing beats a personal appointment. Depending on your potential mentor, that strategy may or may not be practical. If you can't make an appointment to see her or him, the next best thing is a phone call. Use a letter only when you have failed to get a meeting or make the contact by phone. Regardless of

how you make your contact, make it brief and to the point. Any mentor worth his or her salt (unless retired) already has a very busy schedule, and if the prospective mentor thinks future contacts with you are going to take too much time, he or she will either turn your proposal down outright or simply avoid you like the plague.

9. Follow up. After you've made your first contact, follow up with a brief note of appreciation, commenting on something specific that the person said or did.

10. Go to the next person on the list. If your first choice for a mentor turns you down, be sure to find out why. Then go through this same procedure with the next person on your list.

Notebook for Success

Step-by-Step Guide to Recruiting Mentors Who Can Multiply Your Success

INSIGHTS FOR SUCCESS (REVIEW)

Insight 1: A person who believes in you is a tremendous source of power.

Insight 2: Don't be greedy, share the wealth, don't hoard it.

Insight 3: *Who* you work for is as important as *what* you do.

Insight 4: There is no greater motivation than love.

Laws for Achieving Success

Law of Motivation: Expressed appreciation and more money are great motivators.

Law of Relationships: Strive to create "win-win" relationships and deals.

Law of Love: Love *people*. Use *things*. Not vice versa.

Law of Mentors: Be smart. find a mentor (or a coach) to get even smarter.

PERSONAL INVENTORY FOR SUCCESS

1. Using the prioritized list of goals that you created in Chapter 2, and starting with your most important one, make a list of the people you respect most who might be able to give you insight, wisdom, and advice for each goal. List the names in order of preference. In other words, the person at the top of each list should be the person you would choose if you could pick anyone in the world. Even if you don't think there's a prayer of this person giving you a minute of his or her time, that name should be at the top of your list.

2. Create a strategy for approaching and recruiting each of your mentors.

3. Review the relationships and projects you're currently involved in and ask yourself the following questions about each one:

   A. Is it the best win-win situation I can create with those involved? What additional perks could I throw into the pot to make it an even better deal for the other party without significantly hurting my side of the equation?

   B. What are some specific ways that I can express appreciation to the people I relate to at home and on the job?

   C. What kind of negative behavior do I currently impose on others that dishonors them and lowers their self-worth?

   D. What can I do in each of those relationships that will show honor to those I'm relating to, showing that I value them?

   E. If you are having a hard time coming up with specific ideas for C and D, think about the things that other people have said or done to you that you considered demeaning or dishonoring. Think of the things others have done that have made you feel more appreciated and valued.

   F. To acquire more ideas of what you can do to honor those you relate to and increase their self-worth, ask *them* what you can do that would make them feel more appreciated and valued. You might also ask them if there is anything you do that makes them feel *less* valued.

Commitment and Motivation

Two Factors That Are More Important Than Credentials or Resumes

Who in the world would hire these losers, much less give them a big piece of the ownership?

A twenty-seven-year-old corporate failure
A twenty-seven-year-old dog trainer
A twenty-four-year-old oil field worker
A twenty-three-year-old printing estimator
A nineteen-year-old convenience store clerk

No Harvard MBAs. In fact, only one college graduate in the lot. Hardly a formula for building a media empire, yet together they built a dynasty that for twenty years has been the leader in TV mail-order marketing.

INSIGHT 1: COMMITMENT AND MOTIVATION ARE MORE IMPORTANT THAN CREDENTIALS OR RESUMES.

Now the fun starts. I get to tell the story of the company that has been my life for the past twenty years. As I mentioned in the last chapter, it all started with a vision the night in Chicago when Bob Marsh said to me, "If you found a product we could market, we could go into business together and probably make a lot more money selling products than we'll ever make selling TV time."

When Bob made me that offer, I was twenty-seven years old and no major corporation in America would have wanted to hire me if they had studied my resume. But Bob was smart enough to ignore my resume and look at my creativity and my drive. He was also smart enough to know how to motivate me and get me committed to succeeding. But it didn't stop with his attitude toward *me*.

As I pointed out in the previous chapter, our first commercial was so successful that almost overnight we needed managerial help. In a matter of weeks we had gone from zero in sales to $500,000 in sales per *week*. That meant product had to be manufactured, inventoried, and shipped. Television time and print space had to be purchased and managed. And people had to be hired to take care of all that. Instead of going out and finding the most experienced, qualified managers possible, Bob hired his two sons and two sons-in-law. All came to the job with experience but not the kind of experience personnel departments consider applicable. None of the four had an MBA or, for that matter, a college degree. The oldest was twenty-seven and the youngest was nineteen. Their experience? Here's a summary:

John Marsh, 27, Bob's elder son

After high school he served in the Marine Corps reserve where he learned discipline, diligence, and teamwork. Then he operated a commercial fishing ship off the coast of South America where he learned courage and how to survive terrible storms, mutinous crews, and other horrors that made me cringe. After that he started a dog grooming and training service, and, finally, he cofounded a company called Invisible Fence.

With no MBA, no college degree, and no experience in a major corporation, John would never have been considered by a sophisticated personnel department for even a lower-level management position. Yet within a year he was the number two man in the company, which by then was doing $30 million in annual sales. He was the company's main administrator, working with Bob to handle the millions of details not handled in the specific operational areas managed by the rest of us. Today, he is our president.

David Marsh, 24, Bob's younger son

After graduating from high school, Dave did a brief stint in the Naval Reserve. He then worked in the oil and gas fields of western Pennsylvania, supervising a field crew. When he started to work with us, his first responsibility was setting up the manufacturing and fulfillment operations for our first product. He was also responsible for coordinating our efforts with the inbound 800 telephone answering services that would be handling our orders. With virtually no background or experience in any of these areas, he just went out and did it. When our national campaign began in November, our first product instantly became the number one acne medication on the market. Each week twenty-five thousand phone orders were taken, manufactured, and shipped to the consumer on time, thanks to Dave. In less than three months he had set up everything from order taking to customer delivery, and this was before the days of personal computers and without the help of adequate computerization.

Once these systems were set up and operating, Dave took over another area of the company: media buying. Our success was primarily dependent on two factors: our ability to create commercials that could move the consumer from his couch to his phone to order our products, and our ability to buy large blocks of television time at reduced prices from hundreds of television stations. Remove either of these elements, and our business would collapse. Dave became the master at knowing how much to pay for every time-buy on every station. During the last twenty years he has built priceless relationships with the cable networks and television stations, and he oversees the efforts of our sixteen media buyers. He is the best negotiator in the business because he knows how to create an agreement that is a great deal for a station or network and a great deal for us at the same time.

Harry Howard, 23, Bob's elder son-in-law

Harry started working with Bob right after Bob acquired the Ambassador buying account. After high school, his only work experience had been as an estimator for a large printing firm in New Jersey. Harry began by working with Bob and me in the management of Ambassador's TV campaign. When we went into the TV mail-order insurance business in 1977, Harry coordinated our efforts with the three insurance companies who were our joint-venture partners. Due to insurmountable personal conflicts, Harry left our company in 1989.

Edward Shipley, 19, Bob's younger son-in-law

Ed came to us after dropping out of college his freshman year. His only experience was as a convenience-store clerk, a job he had been fired from a few months earlier. When Ed started, nobody had any idea where he would fit in. The result was that he began fitting in wherever there was a need, which was just about everywhere. One day I invited Ed to go to Los Angeles with me to assist with the production of a series of new commercials. He was twenty at the time and had never been on a soundstage. It took only a single trip for him to decide that this was the area he wanted to specialize in. Little did I know that Ed was gifted with tremendous creativity. And his creativity wasn't his only asset. He had the same kind of tenacity and drive I had. He had no problem with the staggeringly long hours of shooting and editing.

He also had a gift that I didn't have: a tremendous drive to experiment with different creative approaches. In a very short time his technical knowledge and expertise in filmmaking surpassed mine. Today, he writes, directs, and produces commercials and infomercials for our company. His efforts have resulted in more than $200 million in sales.

I share these backgrounds of the initial partners in our company to prove resumes and experience are not the most important factors in putting together a business-building team. Far more important is the degree of motivation and the commitment of each partner to the other partners and to the success of the company. I'm not so foolish as to say that experience and intelligence are totally unimportant, but they simply are not as important as motivation and commitment.

INSIGHT 2: IT IS IMPOSSIBLE TO OVERESTIMATE THE INCREDIBLE WORTH OF THE RIGHT PARTNERS.

Law of Partnerships: The power of a few good partners is infinitely greater than the power of a sole proprietor.

If someone offered to bankroll a new business that you wanted to start, and you had the choice of owning it all by yourself or recruiting partners and giving up the majority of your stock, keeping only 20 to 30 percent for yourself, which option would you choose? I am completely convinced that the wrong partners aren't worth a single percentage point, while the right partners are worth 70 or 80! Obviously, there are multimillionaires who have made it on their own without giving up a single point to a partner. If you can achieve your goals that way, more power to you.

But most of us aren't great at everything. Try to find one great administrator who is a marketing whiz, or one marketing whiz who is a great administrator. Believe me, it's not easy. A true marketing whiz is obsessed with marketing and therefore will rarely dedicate the time it takes to administer the details of a business. And an administrator is usually driven to see that every detail of an operation is adequately managed, effectively and efficiently. How can the two be contained in one mind and body? If you find someone who does both, he will either do one well and the other poorly, or simply achieve mediocrity in both. So for most of us, the only way we will ever make it big is if we join up with the right partners.

If I had to focus on any area of our business other than marketing and production, I would finish only one project a year instead of four or five. But because I have great partners who cover every important aspect of our operation, I don't have to spend my time thinking about anything other than what I do best, and the same is true for each of my partners.

You might ask, "Why not own 100 percent of the business and just employ the experts and managers you need?" The answer is that most of us can't afford to hire the best talent in the early years and, equally important, nothing motivates a person to achieve his or her maximum potential like ownership. *Nothing!* Our company is living proof. There are many bigger companies in the United States, but I know of none that is more productive.

And now for the hard part. Notice that the insight for this section is "It is impossible to overestimate the incredible worth of the right partners." Unfortunately, it's a lot easier to find the wrong partners than the right partners. The wrong partner can destroy a business opportunity just as fast as the right partner can build it. So how do you find the right partner? At the end of this chapter is a concise review and plan for doing just that: Strategies and Tips for Identifying and Recruiting the Right Partners.

For myself, I did it the easy way: The right partner found me. I would never have had the wisdom, insight, or maturity back then to pick him, but fortunately Bob Marsh made *me* the offer of partnership. But as I thought about the problem, I realized there are certain steps you can take to find the right partner.

The first step is to assess your own strengths and weaknesses. What you don't need is a carbon copy of yourself. You need someone who has strengths to offset your weaknesses, and talents in areas where you have little or none. This may sound obvious, but I know of quite a few cases where partnerships failed to be productive or failed altogether because people with like talents, strengths, and weaknesses were joined together. So before you can find a good partner, you have to have a realistic appraisal of yourself.

The next step is to identify the talents, abilities, and strengths that you need in a partner to compensate for the areas of your weaknesses and inabilities.

To illustrate these first two steps: My strengths are in the areas of sales, marketing, and persuasion. My weaknesses are in the areas of administration and follow-through on details. I see the upside opportunity in almost any situation but I may be slow to see its realistic downside. In the infant and adolescent stage of our business, therefore, I really didn't need a partner with marketing or sales ability. I needed a partner (or, in my case, partners) who could identify and manage the millions of details necessary in administering the areas of our business other than sales and marketing. As our business grew, a need did arise for an additional partner who could duplicate what I could do because our marketing opportunities were far greater than one person could handle.

So once you have identified the strengths you need in a partner or partners, what other elements are critical in selecting the right partners and avoiding the wrong ones? The first thing you want to look for is a person who shares the same vision you have for your business venture. The person needs not only to see it but also to be overwhelmed by it. He or she needs to want to see it fulfilled as badly as you do. You may have to be the one who communicates that vision—which takes a lot of quality preparation—but if you really have a vision, you can probably communicate it.

In my case, Bob and I were both overcome by the same vision that first day we saw the test results coming in for the handbag. He caught the vision first, but as soon as he stated it, I saw it and became obsessed by it. I knew I had to find a product that he and I could market on television.

The next thing you have to look at is the character and integrity of your would-be partner. These are a lot harder to identify than talents, but they are far more important. If the person's ethics and morals aren't extremely high, there's a pretty good chance that sooner or later that person will betray you or someone else in your company or your customer.

One of my closest friends had a partnership with an extremely talented man. In a few short years they built a great securities business. Unknown to my friend, however, his partner began practicing highly unethical and technically illegal activities relating to some of their customers. His activities were finally discovered by the SEC, and both partners nearly lost everything. The unethical partner lost his license and the business, while my friend barely saved the remaining operation. The character flaw of his partner cost my friend not only a tremendous amount of money but also several years of mental turmoil and anguish.

The next quality to look for in your would-be partner is the willingness to be totally committed to your vision in order to achieve its success. If you are totally committed and your partner isn't, I can promise you that the partnership won't last long. You'll be putting in eighty hours a week, and your partner will be putting in forty. If his or her side of the business requires only thirty and he or she puts in forty, that's great. But the launching stage of a new business normally requires lots of blood, sweat, tears, and time on the part of all the partners.

Remember that the first insight of this chapter is "Commitment and motivation are more important than credentials or resumes." Your partner should be committed not only to your vision but also to you personally. Look at how he or she has performed in other situations. Were his or her commitments short-lived or "faithful until the end"? Is he or she a positive person or a negative person? Negative people are usually very poor partners. Your partner doesn't have to be as positive or as optimistic as you, but if he or she is quick to tear down others or find the negative in situations, when the going gets tough, that person is likely to jump ship or, worse, steer it in the wrong direction.

And last but not least, you should look at your would-be partner's natural drive and gifts rather than his or her resume. Is the person a theorist or a doer? A good many of the MBAs I've met over the years (especially in the big companies I've worked for) are great theorists, but I would no more start a business with them than I would with my German shepherd. In fact, I'd be more likely to start a business with my German shepherd because at least she has a good gut instinct.

The MBAs in the companies I used to work for seemed to be great at explaining things, but if they had to start a business from scratch and make it work with anything less than a few million dollars, I don't think one of them would have had a prayer.

How do you know if your would-be partner is a doer? It's simple: Look at what the person has personally done—not what he has had other people do. For example, if you need a great salesman, don't look at someone who was a salesman once but for the past ten years has been a sales manager. If you need a marketing partner, look for someone who has personally created a marketing campaign—even if it was for a two-bit business—not a person who has simply managed the marketing activities of others. Whatever the person's field, he or she needs to be someone who has no fear of getting into the trenches and doing whatever it takes to win the battle.

Other than Bob, none of the original partners in our company had any significant experience, but we had all worked our butts off in our different jobs and Bob knew we weren't afraid of work. He knew that each of us was resourceful enough to overcome whatever obstacles might fall in our paths. He looked harder at our natural drive than at our talents and abilities.

Finally, make sure that you and your partner are in the same ship, rowing in the same direction. In other words, you both reap the rewards if your venture is successful, and you both suffer if you fail. If one's reward is primarily on the profit side while the other's reward is primarily on the salary side, you will be rowing in different directions. If one is more concerned about the short term while the other is more concerned about the long term, you will be rowing in different directions. It is critical that all the partners row in the same direction.

In our case, we all draw minimal salaries, and more than 90 percent of our income comes from the profits derived in our business. Consequently, when it comes to assessing long- and short-term risks and opportunities, we all have the same motivation. If one of us was paid a percentage of gross sales while the others were paid a percentage of profits, the attitude of the one would be: "I don't care how much it costs us to make the sales as long as we maximize sales." The others would have the attitude: "Don't spend whatever it takes to make the sale but make the sale with as little expenditure as possible."

INSIGHT 3: DO EVERYTHING YOU CAN TO MAKE THOSE YOU WORK WITH SUCCESSFUL.

More times than not, people are only concerned about making themselves successful—sometimes even at the expense of others in their company. Whether it's because they are focused on their own efforts or because they feel a threat from their colleagues, the results are the same. The overall short-term and long-term success of their department or company is impaired.

In our case, we had a man at the top who was not only focused on the overall success of our business but was also committed to seeing each one of us achieve success in our respective areas. How committed was Bob? Ed Shipley was the nineteen-year-old who came to us after having been fired as a convenience-store clerk. Ed had decided he wanted to work in my end of the business. For a few years he traveled with me and was involved in a lot of my production activity. Then the day came for his first production. He stepped up to the plate and struck out. His first project failed—as did his second, third, fourth, fifth, sixth, seventh, eighth, ninth, tenth, eleventh, twelfth, thirteenth, and fourteenth. Fourteen projects, fourteen failures. Those fourteen consecutive failures cost us more than $750,000. If he had been working for any other company in America, he would have been history after the first or second or third. No one would have given him chance number four, much less chance number fifteen! But on chance number fifteen he "hit a triple" and made us a couple of million dollars. And he didn't stop there. In the past six years he has hit home run after home run, resulting in gross sales of close to $200 million and many millions in profits.

I'd pay $750,000 in losses any day for millions in profits. All of us, including Ed, were committed to one another. Even though we had plenty of disagreements, our commitment was greater than our discord.

This commitment to see one another succeed didn't stop with the partners. We have done everything we can to help our employees and even our suppliers and subcontractors be successful. A young man who was a grip on my film projects fifteen years ago is now one of the most capable producers in

Hollywood, and my right arm in production. Actually, he's my whole body! If I didn't have Frank, I would be able to turn out only one or two productions a year, at most. Instead, we can easily produce four or five.

My first assistant, who came on board in 1986, has also turned into an extremely capable producer and is now Ed Shipley's coproducer. My second assistant has become a marketing expert in her own right. Among other things, Patty has helped create and develop two of our company's product lines, which have generated more than $300 million in sales.

Three years ago, Jim McFadden, one of our partner's sons-in-law, came into our business to assist John Marsh in operations. Today, even though he graduated from college with a degree in psychology, he is our vice president of operations, and I wouldn't trade him for any other operations man in America. Jim Shaughnessy came to our company in 1988 with an excellent track record in sales and no experience in manufacturing. We didn't need a salesman; we needed someone who could oversee and manage the small number of manufacturing subcontractors who were making products for us. Today, he is a partner and oversees hundreds of contract manufacturers. Like all of our partners, I would pit him against any manufacturing VP in America.

It is true that everyone in our company who has been successful has achieved that success in large part because of all the others in the company. And it all started at the top, with Bob Marsh being totally committed to seeing his partners and employees reach their upper limits of achievement.

INSIGHT 4: SHARE THE WINNINGS WITH THE PLAYERS.

Law of Mutual Success: Make those under your authority successful and you'll get an incredible ride on top of their rocket.

The final insight in this chapter is one that looks easy on paper but is a lot harder in reality than it looks. As I stated earlier, in 1976 all of us would gladly have gone to work for Bob for a salary. We all would have worked hard in the early years, but would we have worked as hard or been as creative if our entire futures were not on the line? Would it have lasted for twenty years? Would the company have grown to its current position in our industry or in terms of profitability or productivity? Absolutely not!

I've been told by one of our nation's leading motivators that the two strongest motivations in life are the desire for gain and the fear of loss. Owning a piece of the company serves as a two-way motivation: There's a built-in carrot and stick. As an owner, you get tremendously wealthy *if* the company succeeds. If the company fails, you stand to lose everything—and I mean everything. For the first twelve years, each of the partners had to sign personally for the money our company borrowed (millions of dollars), and we also had to pledge as collateral our houses and everything else we owned. If our business went under, we would lose everything we had worked for our entire lives. Twice, in 1985 and again in 1987, this greatest of fears was almost realized. But this fear was a tremendous motivation to be creative and resourceful.

Bob's decision to give us a piece of the action, as incredibly loving and generous as it was, was also a reflection of his logic and intuition. It paid off for him, his family, his partners, his employees, and all of our company's wonderful suppliers and contractors. As you'll see in Chapter 9, sharing the winnings applies to those you work with outside the company as well. Sharing the winnings on the inside means lavish bonuses for company employees in profitable years as well as generous profit-sharing plans. It also means generous salaries for those who make the most significant contributions.

The flip side of sharing the winnings is letting everyone

know that in times of low company profits, there will be lower bonuses and less profit sharing. Not only does everyone end up rowing in the same direction, everybody ends up "cheering" everyone else on. And of course the two greatest motivations mentioned earlier work their magic in everyone from the partners to the newest employees.

STRATEGIES AND TIPS FOR IDENTIFYING AND RECRUITING THE <u>RIGHT</u> PARTNERS

1. Assess your own strengths and weaknesses. What you don't need is a partner who is a carbon copy of yourself.
2. Identify the talent, abilities, and strengths that you need in a partner to compensate for the areas of your weaknesses, inabilities, and lack of interest.
3. Look for a person who shares the same vision you have for your business venture. Your partner not only needs to see it, he needs to be overwhelmed by it.
4. Look at the character and integrity of your would-be partner. This is a lot harder to identify than talents, but it's far more important. If his or her ethics and morals aren't extremely high, sooner or later there's a pretty good chance that person will betray you, someone else in your company, or your customer.
5. Look for a partner who is willing to be totally committed to your vision to achieve its success. If you are totally committed and your partner isn't, I can promise you that the partnership won't last long. Look at how the person has performed in other situations where he or she has been committed. Were those commitments short-lived or faithful until the end?
6. Is the person positive or negative? Negative people are usually very poor partners. A partner doesn't have to be as positive or as optimistic as you, but if that person is

quick to tear down others or find the negative in situations, he or she is likely to jump ship when the going gets tough or, worse, steer the ship in the wrong direction.

7. Look at your would-be partner's natural drive and gifts rather than his or her resume. Is the person a theorist or a doer? How do you know if your partner is a doer instead of a theorist? It's simple: Look at what the person has done personally—not what he has had other people do.

Notebook for Success

Enlisting Partners Who Lower Risk and Increase Potential

INSIGHTS FOR SUCCESS (REVIEW)

Insight 1: Commitment and motivation are more important than credentials or resumes.

Insight 2: It is impossible to overestimate the incredible worth of the right partners.

Insight 3: Do everything you can to make those you work with successful.

Insight 4: Share the wealth.

Laws for Achieving Success

Law of Partnerships: The power of a few good partners is infinitely greater than the power of a sole proprietor.

Law of Mutual Success: Make those under your authority successful, and you'll get an incredible ride on top of *their* rocket.

PERSONAL INVENTORY FOR SUCCESS

1. Looking at each of your goals, write down the names of those who share your vision for each goal. (For example, my wife shares my goals for my being the best husband and father I can be. My two best friends share my goals for growth in my relationship with God. My business partners share my business goals.) If you have a goal for a business project, make a list of the people who share the same goal or those to whom you could communicate your vision for that goal. Once again, put at the top of the list the people you would choose if you could recruit anyone in the world to be your partner in that project.

On any given project, joining up with two good partners can create ten times the potential that joining up with one good partner can create. When possible, on projects or goals that are extremely important to you, try to recruit at least two good partners. The single greatest factor that will determine the heights or the limits of your success is the partners you pick.

2. Begin to explore the ways you can help those who are under your authority at home or at work to become more successful. Become familiar with their goals so you can help them achieve those goals. If they have set no goals, help them to define their goals and to prioritize them. Once you learn what they consider their most important goals, have a brainstorming session together. Try to think of ways you can help them achieve their goals. It may be as simple as an occasional encouraging word. Just as you need a mentor or a coach, so do those under your authority.

CHAPTER 6

"That Woman in the Supermarket"

The Critical Foundation of Selling or Persuading

The best consumer marketing philosophy: Every shopper is the smartest shopper in the world.

INSIGHT 1: CONSUMERS ARE A LOT SMARTER THAN YOU THINK.

Although I believe a college education is in anyone's best interest, I have already admitted that there were only four or five courses out of the forty or so I took that made a contribution to my career. One of the biggest contributions didn't even come from a professor but from a guest lecturer. My favorite professor had brought in Fairfax Cone, a principal in the ad agency Foote, Cone and Belding. I recall nothing from Mr. Cone's forty-five-minute lecture except a comment that became the core of my entire marketing philosophy. It sounds so basic that you may think it's "no big deal."

And yet it has been a key to the track record of my ads—a track record that to my knowledge is unequaled in mail-order marketing.

Here's what Mr. Cone said in that classroom twenty-six years ago: "Ladies and gentlemen, if you forget everything else I say today and remember only this, you'll have a good shot at success in advertising: *'That woman in the supermarket isn't an idiot, she's your wife! And she's the smartest shopper in the world. There are thirty thousand items on the supermarket shelves, and when one of them goes up a nickel, she knows it. So when you're writing your ads, don't treat her like an idiot, treat her with the respect she deserves!'*"

Law of Respect: The more you respect your buyer, the more your buyer will buy.

It sounds so simple. And yet, think about all the ads you've seen that blatantly defy this principle. Remember, just because you see a commercial or infomercial on TV or an ad in print, don't assume that it is successful. A lot more ads *fail* than succeed in selling the consumer.

From my perspective there are only two types of advertising: conventional and direct response or mail order. Conventional advertising is intended to help you make a buying decision at a future time or at a place of purchase, such as a store, a car dealership, and so forth. This represents the vast majority of advertising you are confronted with on a daily basis. Direct-response or mail-order advertising asks you to place an order directly from the ad, either by calling or mailing in your order.

WHY MOST CONVENTIONAL COMMERCIALS AND ADS FAIL OR AREN'T AS SUCCESSFUL AS THEY COULD BE

1. The people creating the ads use the wrong definition or criterion of success. There are many successful conventional commercials and advertisements; however, there are far more unsuccessful ones. The ultimate success of any ad should be measured only by sales; that is, does it cause the reader, viewer, or listener to choose one company's goods or services over another's.

As simple as this concept is, judging an ad's success by sales alone would terrify most ad agencies. I'd like to meet an agency that would say to a client, "Hey, if my ads don't increase your sales, don't pay me." Or how about: "You don't have to pay me for the ad, just give me a percentage of the increase in sales I create." Unfortunately, most ad agencies would quickly go broke if they made that kind of offer.

Instead, ad agencies' definition of a successful ad is one that increases brand or product awareness. They would defend this position by saying, "Sales are dependent on too many factors other than advertising (such as pricing, product quality, shelf space and location, sales promotions, sales force, and so on); therefore, it's wrong to hold advertising accountable for sales increases or decreases." While they are right that there are many factors other than advertising that influence sales, they are wrong to surrender accountability so quickly.

They also embrace their definition of success because it's much easier to create awareness and recall (or memorability) than it is to create additional sales. By creating a lower standard by which success is measured, the agencies can claim success more often and much more easily. Even a child can be a successful high-jumper when the bar is only six inches off the ground.

Corporate managers, wake up! If your sales don't improve in a stagnant or increasing market, or don't remain steady in a shrinking market, fire your agency and look for one that can sell. Don't be a co-conspirator with your agency by accepting *their* low standards of successful advertising.

2. The people creating the ads are often influenced by the wrong motives. In broadcasting, all commercials are created by writers, producers, and directors. Sometimes their sole motive is to create commercials that sell the client's products. But more often than not, other motives creep into their thinking and significantly alter the direction and outcome of their work. They want their work to be viewed by their bosses and the client as "imaginative" or "creative" or "spectacular" or "moving," and so forth.

Their thoughts are often more geared to how the commercial will look on their demo reel. (A demo reel is a collection of a person's productions on videotape that allows prospective employers to see the quality and character of the work.) Most writers, directors, and producers of commercials would love to make the leap from commercials to a television series or to feature films, the ultimate leap. Even though these may not be their prime motivations, they are often present and consequently influence significantly the outcome of their work.

Another motive is the lavish budgets dedicated to production. Many agencies are compensated with commissions on production. In other words, the more they spend on a production, the more money they make, so they create spectacular commercials that cost a fortune.

Still, more often than not, spectacular, wonderful, beautiful, imaginative, creative ads don't persuade the consumer nearly as well as simple, logical, less expensive ads do.

3. The people creating the ads do not have an adequate or direct measurement of the impact current or past ads have made on sales.

Because there are so many factors that affect sales, it is extremely difficult to measure precisely the impact of any one conventional ad or ad campaign on sales. And if it is so hard to measure the impact of an individual ad, it's next to impossible to measure individual elements of an ad, such as the impact of a particular word or sentence, or one actor or spokesman versus another. And yet an ad's effectiveness is the sum total of the effectiveness of all of the individual elements that make up that ad plus the ad's overall impression. If you can't precisely measure the sales impact of the individual elements and the ad as a whole, how can you learn what sells and what doesn't? The answer is, you can't!

4. Since the people creating the ads can't measure the impact of their past ads and the individual elements of those ads, they can't make educated revisions and adjustments to their new ads to create an even greater impact on sales.

These are without a doubt the two greatest roadblocks to creating conventional advertising that will maximize sales. They are the two reasons an experienced mail-order writer can outsell an experienced conventional writer (with no mail-order experience) anytime, any day, with his typewriter (or computer notebook) tied behind his back. And with every ad a mail-order writer writes, whether the ad fails or succeeds, he becomes a little bit smarter and a little bit better at selling.

Law of Testing: Survey for "ballparks"; test for "home runs."

One of the great advantages of mail-order marketing over other forms of marketing is the ability of the marketer to rely on market tests rather than on market surveys and focus groups. A survey or focus group can point a marketer in a general direction and possibly place him in the right "ballpark," but that's all it can do. On the other hand, a well-constructed market *test* gives a marketer enough precise detail to forecast accurately the future results of a marketing campaign.

The late Art DeMoss was CEO of the mail-order insurance company I worked for in the early 70s (National Liberty Corporation). Because NLC had the largest advertising budget of any life insurance company in America, a lot of the big agencies would send in their best account teams to try to win a piece of the account. Art always had fun pulling out loose-leaf binders with copies of all the various ads the company had tested over the years. He would ask the account executives to look at the ads and tell him which ones generated the most sales and which ones sold the least. Every page had two or three ads that had been tested against each other, head to head. Without exception the agency executives always picked the prettiest, the most "creative," and the "slickest" ads. And every time they were wrong. They didn't have a clue as to what sold and what didn't, much less why one would outsell the others. And yet in their arrogance they thought they were going to move right in and take this fat account away from the much smaller mail-order ad agencies that had been with Art from the beginning. Wrong!

5. Conventional advertising usually doesn't have enough time in a commercial or enough space in a print ad to sell a product adequately.

To use a television commercial to really "sell" a product requires more than thirty seconds of time. Likewise, a magazine ad usually requires at least a full page of advertising. You not only need more time and space than most conventional advertising allocates but you also need to know what to *do* with it. This brings me back to what Fairfax Cone said twenty-six years ago, the basis of my marketing and selling philosophy, namely, treating your consumers with respect means giving them logical reasons to choose your product or service. And in broadcasting, that takes time; in print, it takes space.

INSIGHT 2: ARTISTIC SWELLS. LOGIC SELLS.

Most of the commercial writers and directors I have met think of themselves as artists, so they try to create commercials and ads that show off their "creative" or "artistic" flair. As a result, most of their ads contain more art than "sell." Their hope is to win an award or at least have people "oooo" and "ah." So their ads result in "swelled" heads and egos. On the other hand, there's really no art in logic. Logic is best conveyed in a simple, straightforward manner. Logical ads win few, if any, awards and swell no one's ego, but boy do they sell!

At one point early in our corporate history I was so busy creating new projects and commercials that my partners thought it might help if we found a good mail-order writer who could take some of the magazine advertising load off my shoulders. We went to one of the top mail-order writers on Madison Avenue, gave him a product that we were already selling in print, and asked him to write an ad. We told him to give it his best shot because if it generated sales equal to or greater than the ad I had written, we would throw a lot of work his way. We gave him the product and all of the information we had about it, but we did not give him a copy of my ad. Four weeks later he submitted his ad.

I was fairly young at the time, and when I saw his ad, I felt sick. It was so much more creative than mine; it made me look like I had no creative talents at all. I was convinced it would generate a lot more orders than my ad would. Mine was very logical and followed the very dry formula I had developed. His had a snazzy headline and a wonderful flair. To make matters even harder on my ego, all my partners (except Bob Marsh) thought his was a *lot* better than mine.

We ran a perfect head-to-head test in *Parade* magazine. Before the ads ran, Bob could tell I was pretty discouraged. He came up to me the day before the ad ran and said, "You know what I think? I think your ad is going to blow the other one away." My ears perked up and my heart started to race. Oh, how I love Bob Marsh! "You really think so?" I asked. "Yep. Not even a question," he said. I didn't give him a hug, but I sure wanted to.

Both ads ran the next day, and the orders started pouring in. To my relief (and education), logic and my formula won—and won big! My ad outpulled the seasoned pro's, not by a few percentage points but by five to one! Needless to say, my partners never again suggested turning to another writer. (By the way, remember that their intention was fine. They were trying to find a way to relieve some of my workload and the pressure that went with it.) Even though the success of my ad meant I was going to have to continue working at a blistering pace, I was happy to know that I could go head-to-head against the most seasoned pros and win. I had a genuine need to feel that my work was good, and, perhaps the best. I needed to feel that way then (twenty years ago), and I still need to feel that way now.

Law of Building: Don't start building the house until you've laid the foundation.

So how do you use logic to sell? You start by asking yourself logical questions about your product and your offer.

- What are all the benefits associated with my product? (Make this list as long and as detailed as possible. Include all major benefits, minor benefits, side benefits, and so forth.)
- How does my product relate to my consumers' two greatest motivations—the desire for gain and the fear of loss?
- What makes my product different from competing products?
- How can I raise the perceived value of my product without significantly raising my price?

- In light of all the facts (cost of goods, cash flow, competitive prices and offers), what is the best offer I can make my consumer (pricing, payment terms, rebates, volume discounts, premiums, and so forth)?
- How can I improve the consumer's perception of my product (awareness, credibility, quality, value)?

Next, ask yourself logical questions about your consumer.

- Who is my primary consumer, and what percentage of my market does he or she represent? (Consider sex, age range, socioeconomic demographics, geographical location, et cetera.)
- What are the primary and secondary motivations for this consumer to buy the type or class of product I'm selling? What does the consumer desire to gain by purchasing the product, and what potential loss might the consumer experience by not purchasing the product?
- What objections and excuses might this consumer use to delay or avoid a buying decision about this product?
- What answers or rebuttals to each of these objections and excuses can you offer?
- Who is your secondary consumer? Go through the above questions with him or her in mind.

Once you have answered these questions, you have all the raw data you need to create your approach to make a logical sale, whether you want to make the sale orally, in writing, or through a formal advertisement. Your next step is to take your responses and order them according to importance; for example, prioritize your product's benefits, your consumer's objections and excuses, and their potential motivations for buying.

When you have finished prioritizing, you can then tailor your message to deal with the most important things first and the less important later. Notice that I didn't say "last." You should never end any sales effort, whether a verbal presentation or an advertisement, by dealing with the least important benefits or objections or excuses. To do so makes you look as if you are so anxious to close the sale that you're reaching for straws. To the contrary, the end of any sales effort should be a summary of the most important benefits and should overcome the biggest objections and excuses.

All of this sounds so basic and simple that you must be thinking it's no big deal. If you're a competitor of mine, please keep thinking that way. It really is no big deal, but it works. I've used it for every product I've ever marketed and every commercial and ad I have ever written. It's the foundation. By definition foundations usually aren't pretty and creative. They are dull slabs of concrete. But try to build a great house without a good foundation, and you'll fail miserably. To take shortcuts or spare effort or time when laying the foundation is a fool's shortcut to failure.

STRATEGIES AND TIPS FOR CREATING IRRESISTIBLE SALES PRESENTATIONS AND AD CAMPAIGNS

Lori Davis Hair Care Products

Scenario: On any given day, the most famous faces in Hollywood can be seen walking into a secret room (not open to the public) in a little known Los Angeles hair salon. Cher, Julia Roberts, Michelle Pfeiffer, Winona Ryder, Arnold Schwarzenegger, Ted Danson, Danny DeVito, Larry Hagman, and more than a hundred others are the regular clients of Lori Davis. She's not a hair stylist, she is Hollywood's leading hair colorist and conditioner. She is known as Hollywood's hair doctor and is considered a miracle worker by her clients. The movie studios pay her as much as $3,000 a day to make their stars' hair look its absolute best. She does this with the skill of a brain surgeon, the artistry of a Rembrandt, and an array of amazing products she has created with hair chemists to meet the specific needs of her celebrity clients. Her products, depended on and devoured by her clients, have never been made available to the public. They are incredibly effective and equally expensive.

After meeting and spending a good deal of time with Lori, we decided to create an infomercial and offer her products to the public. Below is a copy of the logical lists that served as a foundation to the campaign I was going to create—a campaign that resulted in the fastest growing hair care line in history, selling over $100 million of product in its first two years.

I. Product Benefits

A. *Perfection* Deep Conditioner
  1. Reconstructs damaged hair
  2. Shields hair from damage due to environmental problems and chemical treatments
  3. Radically reduces appearance of split ends
  4. Adds noticeable shine to hair
  5. Adds noticeable volume to hair
  6. Makes hair much more manageable and controllable
  7. Doesn't weigh hair down
  8. Moisturizes hair

B. *Memory Hold* Hair Spray
  1. Holds hair in place without stickiness or "glueing" effect of conventional hair sprays
  2. No more "helmet head" feeling or look

C. *Crystalline Shine*
  1. Adds instant shine to hair
  2. Reduces appearance of split ends

D. Lori's Shampoos
 1. Add volume to hair
 2. Cleanse the hair without conditioning it
 3. Three separate shampoos tailored for normal to oily hair, color-treated hair, or dry, damaged hair

E. Lori's Weekly Clarifier
 1. Cleanses all impurities and deposits left behind by ordinary shampoos
 2. Eliminates the need to change shampoos every few months

F. Lori's Products in Combination as a System
 1. Eliminate "bad hair days"
 2. Make hair look better than it has ever looked
 3. Enable user to look great and feel more confident about appearance
 4. Eliminate worry and panic about hair

II. Consumer Motivators

1. Desire for gain: Hair will look better than ever. Won't have to worry about hair looking bad. Won't have to worry about a man's hand getting "stuck" when he runs his fingers through it.
2. Fear of loss: If I don't try this product, my hair will never look as good as it could, and I will continue to have bad hair days.

III. Product Differentiation

1. Five products create a fabulous hair care system.
2. Three shampoos for specific hair type.

3. Shampoos *don't* contain conditioners that weigh the hair down or leave the hair limp.
4. Shampoos *do* contain moisturizers to prevent dry hair.
5. Shampoos are "color safe."

IV. Perceived Value: How can I improve the perceived value of my product without significantly raising the price?

1. Include an instructional and styling video. Manufactured cost: $2.00; perceived value: $39.95.
2. Show Lori's salon prices of each product in kit.
3. Name celebrities that use product.
4. Get celebrity testimonies.
5. Use higher quality packaging than anyone else uses for hair care products.
6. Have Lori explain that she used highest-price ingredients because her celebrity clients wanted the best products, and these products were created for them.
7. Add up individual salon prices of products in kit and use that price as the comparison for the kit.

V. Best Offer: In light of all the facts (cost of goods, cash flow, competitive prices and offers) what is the best offer I can make my consumer?

(pricing, payment terms, rebates, volume discounts, premiums, and so forth) and still meet my gross profit margin objectives?

1. $120 value
2. Only 2 payments of $19.95
3. Free videotape
4. Thirty-day money-back guarantee

VI. Raising the Consumer's Perception: How can I raise the consumer's perception of my product (awareness, credibility, quality, value)?

1. Celebrity endorsements
2. Price comparison
3. Before and after pictures
4. User testimonials
5. Explanation of what each product does and why it does it so well
6. Which celebrity uses which product and why

VII. Logical Questions About the Potential Consumer of This Product

QUESTION   *Who* is my primary consumer, and what percentage of my market does he or she represent (sex, age range, socioeconomic demographics, geographical location, and so forth)?

ANSWER   Female credit card holders ages twenty to fifty, middle income and above—85 percent of my market.

QUESTION   What are the primary and secondary motivations for this consumer to buy the type or class of product I'm selling? What does the consumer want to gain by purchasing the product, and what potential loss might the consumer experience by not purchasing the product?

ANSWER   Hair that looks better than it looks now.
The best-looking hair they can possibly have.
Improved overall appearance
Feel better about self
Worry less about hair and appearance.
Great-looking hair fast, with little effort.

QUESTION   What objections or excuses might the consumer use to delay or avoid a buying decision about this product?

ANSWER $40.00 for a set of hair care products is too expensive.

I would never spend that much money on hair care products without trying them first.

Don't need it.

All hair care products are similar; these can't be much different.

How do I know which of the three shampoos to order?

I'd never buy anything from TV.

I'll wait until it's in the stores.

What if I bought it and hated it?

QUESTION   What is the answer to each of these objections and excuses?

ANSWER   Response to "$40.00 for a set of hair care products is too expensive":

A. Purchased separately, you'd pay $120 for these same items.

B. These products are far better than any salon products you've ever bought.

C. Only the best and most expensive ingredients were used to achieve the maximum results because these products were originally created for movie and TV stars who want the absolute best no matter what the cost.

D. The free video included in the kit is worth $40.00 by itself.

Response to "I would never spend that much money on hair care products without trying them first": Money-back guarantee allows you to try all of the products for a full thirty days without any risk. You can return empty bottles for full refund.

Response to "I don't need it": Every woman needs these products to repair hair damaged from chemical treatments, perms, coloring, heat damage, and environmental damage. As hair is repaired, your hair will look noticeably better than it has ever looked.

Response to "All hair care products similar; these can't be much different": These products are radically different from any other products on the market today. Lori's superstar clients have to have their hair looking its best. They can afford any product on the market, but they all look to Lori. Why? Because her products really *are* different!

Response to "How do I know which of the three shampoos to order?": Is your hair naturally dry or dried out from chemical treatments such as perms or coloring? If so, order Lori's moisturizing shampoo. If your hair isn't dried out but is colored, use her shampoo for color-treated hair. If your hair is normal to oily and not color treated, order her shampoo for normal to oily hair.

Response to "I'd never buy anything from TV": This is your chance to buy these products the same way all of Lori's clients do—direct from Lori, without paying store or salon markups.

Response to "I'll wait until it's in stores": It won't be in stores for at least two years, and even then, not *all* of these products may be available.

Response to "What if I bought it and hated it?": You can return it for a full refund. But chances are you're going to love these products just like Lori's celebrity clients. In fact, once you use them, you'll never go back to anything else.

Notebook for Success

Persuading or Selling: Doubling Your Batting Average in Thirty Days

INSIGHTS FOR SUCCESS (REVIEW)

Insight 1: Consumers are a lot smarter than you think.
Insight 2: Artistic swells. Logic sells.

Laws for Achieving Success

Law of Respect: The more you respect your buyer, the more your buyer will buy.
Law of Testing: Survey for "ballparks"; test for "home runs."
Law of Building: Don't start building the house until you've laid the foundation.

PERSONAL INVENTORY FOR SUCCESS

1. Does your ad, sales pitch, or presentation
   treat viewers, readers or hearers with respect?
   lead them along a clear, logical progression?
   clearly play to their two greatest motivations?
   begin and end with the most important reasons for them
     to take the action you're suggesting?
2. If you are communicating orally, are you using clear and applicable "word pictures" in your presentation? (See Strategies and Tips for Powerful Communication at the end of Chapter 11.)
3. Use the steps listed on pages 105–10 to create your "logical" sell.

CHAPTER 7

How to Hit a Lot of Home Runs in Anything You Do

Taking Swings and Lots of Them!

Selling products on TV no one thought could be sold, and selling them in record numbers no one could believe.

Most people who find out that I make my living by writing and directing television commercials and infomercials ask if I went to film school or majored in broadcasting or communications. When I say no, the next question asked is, "Well, how did you learn to do what you do?" The answer is, I didn't learn to do what I do. I just did it. Until Bob and I joined up in 1976, I had never written or produced a single commercial. My only exposure to production was having watched a commercial being produced a few months earlier.

A few weeks after Bob and I had joined forces, we needed to produce a thirty-second commercial for one of Bob's media clients that would call the viewer's attention to an insert in the

Sunday newspaper. I wrote the spot and hired a crew to shoot it. I watched the director instruct the crew, while I directed the talent and coached the dialogue between two actresses. It was a piece of cake.

The first real test came two months later when I had to write and produce our first two-minute direct-response commercial. It was my first real test for three reasons. First, I wouldn't be directing part-time Philadelphia actresses, I would be directing a major celebrity. (Would he trust my direction, or would he recognize my inexperience?) Second, because the setup was "direct response," it wouldn't matter how nice it looked or sounded, or how much we liked it. The only thing that counted was whether or not viewers would go to the phones and order our product. Third, and most important, unlike my first effort which held no real consequences for our company, this commercial would determine whether or not our company would survive. Not only was *my* entire future riding upon the outcome, the careers and well-being of Bob's fifteen employees (though they didn't realize it) was riding on whether or not enough viewers responded to this commercial to roll it into a national campaign. Had I realized at the time that only one in every twenty-five mail-order commercials produced back then succeeded (and that was the rate of the "pros" who knew what they were doing), I would have been terrified. But ignorance was bliss.

As I mentioned in Chapter 4, that first commercial turned out to be a grand slam, producing $20 million in sales in our first year. Its importance didn't stop with the sales or profits it created, however; it gave us enough operating capital to enable us to find more products and to create more commercials to sell those products. Equally important, it resulted in Bob's sons and sons-in-law coming into the partnership, and you already know how important that turned out to be.

Our first product—the acne medication, using Pat Boone

and his then seventeen-year-old daughter Debby as our spokespersons—became the number one selling acne medication its first week on the market in terms of sales and profitability. Considering that it wasn't available in any store in America, that was pretty amazing for a start-up company and product. In fact, the numbers were so amazing that as the word got out, nobody in the pharmaceutical business believed them.

So that was my first trip to the plate. The next two commercials I produced (one was to sell memberships in a buying club and the other sold a high-fiber weight-loss plan) were successful in terms of the response they generated. Unfortunately, the group managing the buying club failed miserably at their end, and the company manufacturing the weight-loss product couldn't manufacture and ship the orders as fast as we were generating them. It was incredibly frustrating to have produced commercials that generated tens of thousands of orders, only to lose money because the companies we were depending on failed to carry out their end of the business.

Even though it was hard on us at the time, that experience turned out to be one of the best things that ever happened to us. We learned the hard way that it wasn't enough to produce winning commercials to sell our products. We had to take charge of every aspect of our business—from quality control in the manufacturing process to managing every detail of product fulfillment, shipping, and customer service.

All of this took place in 1977, and resulted in one of the most important steps in our business history: We started our own fulfillment company to inventory and ship all our orders. I was against this move, figuring we had no idea what we were doing, but John and Dave Marsh insisted.

To handle this job, we hired John Foster, a friend who had no experience in this area but was totally committed to success. We gave him a big piece of the ownership of the fulfillment operation to motivate him. The result? We ended up with the most efficient, best-run mail-order fulfillment operation in America. The speed and cost efficiency of this operation became key to our customer satisfaction and low return rates. Thank goodness my partners prevailed. I doubt that our company could have survived the expense and inefficiencies of the other fulfillment services available to us back then.

During this same period another disaster almost sunk our business. Elvis died. One of our competitors had old commercials on his shelf for the sale of Elvis records. He began running them and generated hundreds of thousands of telephone calls into the 800 answering services so that none of our customers could get through. (These were the days when answering services weren't computerized and couldn't effectively handle anywhere near the volume of calls they can handle today.)

Our only hope was to come up with our own Elvis products. In a matter of a few weeks Ed Shipley and I put together two Elvis packages, one featuring a book that I coauthored. We put them on the air and took 250,000 orders in a matter of weeks.

INSIGHT 1: YOU HAVE TO TAKE A LOT OF SWINGS TO HIT A LOT OF HOME RUNS.

In an industry where the success rate was about 4 percent, I was hitting nearly 50 percent in our first eighteen months. My spots generated more than 3 million telephone orders. We took our first orders in September 1976 and by December 1977 were the leading television mail-order marketers in the country. But despite our successful response rates, we weren't making a ton of money. One project lost a lot of money because of the fulfillment problem. Several others lost money due to high COD refusal rates. (Back then, only 12 percent of our orders used credit cards; the rest were shipped COD.)

In 1977 we sold a lot of product, and we also pioneered a whole new industry. Other companies had tried to use direct-response commercials to sell life insurance but had failed. No wonder: It took the average life insurance salesman three appointments, averaging one to two hours each, to sell a life insurance policy. That being the case, how can you possibly sell a life insurance policy in 120 seconds? Well, as I mentioned in Chapter 3, we did it with the help of Senator Sam Ervin. In the ten years that followed, we generated tens of millions of dollars in insurance premiums, but competitive companies jumped onto the bandwagon and collectively we generated sales of hundreds of millions of dollars.

By 1979 I was shooting nearly a hundred commercials on ten to twenty new products per year. Why so many commercials per product? On nearly every product we were shooting "variations," to test different prices, different spokespersons, different copy approaches, and different offer alternatives. And even though my success rate fell to about 30 percent, with every test we learned more and more. Before long my success rate rebounded to 90 percent, not because we were such "geniuses," but because we did so much testing. To show you the importance of testing *everything,* let me give you a short quiz.

QUESTION You have a new acne product no one has ever heard of. The going price for acne medications in stores is $1.25 to $1.75. You price-test yours at $6.50 and $9.50 per bottle. Which price will generate the most orders?

ANSWER If you guessed the higher price, you were right. It pulled about 25 percent more orders. It seems that when it comes to medications, consumers feel that the higher the price, the more effective the medication. The 25 percent increase in response, combined with a 50 percent higher price, resulted in a 230 percent higher gross margin, and that higher margin gave us the operating budget we needed to pay for a national campaign.

QUESTION   You test three commercials for this same product, one using Pat Boone alone, one using Pat and his wife Shirley, and one with Pat and his daughter Debby (before her hit song). Will there be any difference in the pull? If so, which one will win, and by what percentage?

ANSWER   There was a big difference in the pull! Pat and Debby outpulled the other two by more than 30 percent.

QUESTION   You have two commercials for a telephone headset, featuring Loretta Swit. One offers the headset for $19.95, the other for $24.95. Which one will generate more orders, and by what percentage?

ANSWER   If you were lucky enough to guess the higher price on the acne medication, you guessed right. But if you guessed the higher price on the telephone headset, you guessed wrong—disastrously wrong! The $5.00 difference resulted in a 40 percent drop in response. We made a lot of money at the lower price but would have *lost* a lot of money had we rolled out with the higher price. What's the lesson of these two tests? You can never assume that a price-test winner on one product means you'll see the same results on another product. Thus, you always test pricing. *Always!*

QUESTION   Two commercials feature John Ritter as the spokesman for "Where There's a Will, There's an 'A'" video series. The spots are identical, except for one small paragraph. Spot A has a fourteen-second laundry list of seven specific areas covered in the video series. Spot B has some very strong endorsement statements by John. Which spot won, and by what percentage?

ANSWER   What kind of a difference can a single 14-second paragraph make in a 120-second commercial? The offer, the price, the celebrity, the approach or format, the opening and closing are all the same. How much of a difference can a single piece of copy make? The difference between a big winner and a big loser! In this case the laundry list version won big, while the stronger endorsement version lost big. How big? The winner made millions, and the loser would have lost millions.

QUESTION   You have three commercials selling a unique type of life insurance. You use the exact same script in all three commercials. The only difference is that one uses a "C" celebrity (a has-been celebrity), the second uses a "B" celebrity (a former but recent prime-time TV star with a good image), and the third uses an "A" celebrity, (current prime-time TV star with a good image). How much of a difference is there in viewer response to the three commercials?

ANSWER   The "B" celebrity outpulled the "C" by two to one, and the "A" outpulled the "B" by three to one. So the difference in response between an "A" celebrity and a "C" celebrity was six to one.

Why is this question so important? Because a "C" celebrity costs a lot less money to hire than a "B" celebrity, and a "B" celebrity costs a lot less than an "A" celebrity. So if you can get nearly the same results with a lower-caliber celebrity, why pay for a more expensive one? Remember, all three had the identical script.

This was a test we conducted early on, and it became the basis for our philosophy of going after celebrity endorsements: Always go for the absolute best you can possibly afford. The amazing thing is that at the time we were learning this, there were numerous articles in the various advertising trade publications quoting most of the ad agency experts as saying celebrity endorsers rarely made any significant difference in product sales. Boy, were they wrong! How could all of these high-paid, high-powered advertising geniuses be so wrong?

You'll get that answer in the next chapter where I share some other surprising insights we've learned in using more celebrity endorsers than any other company in America.

The insight for this section was "You have to take a lot of swings to hit a lot of home runs." In our business that amount of testing was possible because in the early years, on average, I would spend $5,000 to $15,000 per commercial. Consequently, I could not only test lots of products, I could test lots of commercial variations for each product. During that same period, conventional ad agencies were spending $250,000 to $1 million to produce thirty-second national spots and couldn't possibly afford to do the variety of testing we did. So they were forced to rely primarily on their marketing research departments, surveys, and focus groups. Those results are about as accurate and projectable as trying to hit a three-foot target from twenty thousand feet with a paper airplane. No wonder they are wrong more often than than they are right. In my opinion, most of the time that they are right, it's because of the broken clock theory. (You know: Even a broken clock is right twice a day.)

During our early years, the products we sold were as diverse as you could imagine. In many cases, each time we entered a new industry, we broke all existing records. For example, a hardcover book would be considered a national best-seller if it sold between five thousand and ten thousand copies per week. In four years we sold fourteen titles, selling a minimum of twenty-five thousand copies per week, per title. On one of the books we hit fifty thousand copies per week. With one exception, all these books were written by totally unknown authors, and yet we sold over $100 million worth in less than four years.

One reporter called and asked us what kind of sales volume we were generating on some of the more notable titles, such as *Too Young to Die*. When we told him, he called several big publishing companies, asking if the numbers we were quoting were possible. We soon received a call from the now "irate" reporter telling us that publishing experts said *nobody* could sell that many copies per week without everyone in the publishing industry knowing about it. As far as they were concerned, achieving those kinds of numbers was nearly impossible, even when using thousands of retail outlets. How could anyone achieve sales like that *without* being on a single retail shelf? But we were glad they all *thought* our numbers were BS. The entire four years we sold books, not one publisher ever ventured into our arena to compete with us—all because they couldn't believe we were really doing what we said we were doing.

Between 1977 and 1986, in addition to books and life insurance policies, we sold a myriad of products, including a skin care line, a weight-loss program, a telephone headset, a woman's notebook planner, a low-cost burglar alarm, and a political magazine. We made a lot of money on some products and lost a lot on others. Most important, we kept learning and applying what we learned. All of this experience came from using two-minute commercials because we had not yet stumbled into the arena of 30-minute "infomercials."

INSIGHT 2: NO RECRIMINATIONS FOR FAILURES.

Law of Recovering: When those near, around, or under you strike out, soothe their pain and disappointment with a listening ear and encouraging words. No criticism at all and no analysis or advice for at least two days. This approach applies to fellow workers, employees, friends, and, most important, family members.

Now it's time for another tribute to my generous partners. During these first ten years, I wrote, directed, and produced more than eight hundred commercials, testing scores of products and many variations of commercials on most of those products. Each year, for every home run I hit, I struck out anywhere from one to four times. And yet my partners never criticized me or my efforts. Never once! Whenever I struck out, they'd always gather around me, pick me up, and encourage me. So instead of dreading my next at-bat, I wanted to go to the plate again and keep swinging for the home runs instead of playing it safe and settling for a walk or a single. Of all the companies I worked for, this was the only one where my failures were met with encouragement instead of recriminations and criticism.

Managers, when your people strike out, don't greet them with a critical or a know-it-all Monday-morning quarterback attitude. Instead, give them all the encouragement you can muster. Remember that they're hurting a lot more from their strikeout than you are. They're getting all the criticism they need from their own minds. When the time is right and they are a few days or a few weeks away from their failure, encourage them to study it and come up with an analysis of the whys behind the failure. We really do learn more from failures than we do from successes. But the time to learn is not when we're reeling and numb, it's when we've gained enough time and distance from it to be objective. Some people may need a few weeks.

> *Law of Analysis: Analyze your strikeouts as soon as the pain and numbness subside.*
> *Law of Strikeouts: After a strikeout, don't hope for a walk or try to bunt or start swinging timidly. Learn from the strikeout, focus on the pitch, and swing for the bleachers.*

And friend, when you strike out and everyone around you wants to tell you why you struck out or criticize you, ask them as nicely as you can to write down their thoughts and give them to you in a couple of days. It will not only help them to be more objective and insightful, it will give you the time you need to get over the initial pain and numbness of the strikeout so you can receive their insights far more objectively.

Isn't it sad that I worked for nine companies before ATC, and not one of them knew how to handle their employees' failures? Babe Ruth was not only baseball's home-run king, he was its strikeout king. Can you imagine what would have happened to his home-run hitting if every time he struck out, he was instantly confronted by his manager and teammates and criticized and analyzed? Most coaches and athletes know better. Why can't corporate America understand such a simple principle?

Notebook for Success
Converting Strikeouts into Home Runs

INSIGHTS FOR SUCCESS (REVIEW)

Insight 1: You have to take a lot of swings to hit a lot of home runs.

Insight 2: No recriminations for failures.

Laws for Achieving Success

Law of Recovery: When those near, around, or under you strike out, soothe their pain and disappointment with a listening ear and encouraging words. No criticism at all, and no analysis or advice for at least two days. This approach applies to fellow workers, employees, friends, and, most important, family members.

Law of Analysis: Analyze your strikeouts as soon as the pain and numbness subside.

Law of Strikeouts: After a strikeout, don't hope for a walk or try to bunt or start swinging timidly. Learn from the strikeout, focus on the pitch, and swing for the bleachers.

PERSONAL INVENTORY FOR SUCCESS

1. How do you normally handle your own strikeouts in business and personal relationships? With anger? Depression? Denial? Rationalization? Or with patience? Seeking of insights from others? Determination and diligence to analyze, discover, and learn? Look at one or more past strikeouts or failures and write down how you responded initially and then over time. Write down what you now believe would have been the best way to respond immediately and over time.

2. How do you normally handle the strikeouts or failures of others in business and in personal relationships? With analysis? Criticism? Advice? Anger? Discipline? Or with encouragement? Comfort? Listening? Patience? Partnership? Look at one or more past strikeouts or failures of others and write down how you responded. (If you can't remember, ask your family or fellow workers. They don't forget as quickly as we do.) Then write down what you now believe would have been the best immediate and longer-term responses.

Shooting for the Moon

The Critical Key to Extraordinary Success in Any Area of Your Life

Good celebrities can't be bought. They have to believe.

In April 1983, I had a product that I thought would be perfect for Tom Selleck. I found out that his agent was Betty McCart and put in a call to her. Her assistant was a young man named John, and he wasn't about to put my call through until he knew what it was about. I told him that I was interested in signing Tom Selleck for a commercial, and he instantly told me that Tom didn't do commercials. I replied that he ought to at least hear my offer before he turned me down. He replied, "You don't understand. It doesn't matter how much your offer is, even if it's ten million dollars. Tom has a flat rule: no commercials." I asked if I could at least talk to Betty, and he replied, "Not if it's about Tom." And with that we said good-bye. Six months later I had another project, even more perfect for Tom, and decided to try one more time to get through to Betty. Here's how it went.

AGENCY: Betty McCart's office. This is John speaking.

ME: John, this is Steve Scott with American Telecast. Is Betty in?

AGENCY: May I ask who this is in reference to?

ME: Tom Selleck.

AGENCY: What about Tom Selleck?

ME: I have an offer for a commercial.

AGENCY: Didn't you call about Tom a few months ago?

ME: That's right.

AGENCY: Look, Steve, I told you then that Tom will not do any commercials, no matter how much you offer, and that's *still* the case. Nothing's changed!

ME: Yeah, but you haven't heard my offer yet.

AGENCY: (interrupting): It doesn't matter if it's ten million or twenty million, he still won't do a commercial.

ME: John, my offer's a lot better than that, and you and Betty really owe it to Tom to take it to him.

AGENCY: What's the offer?

ME: Free. I want him to do it for free!

AGENCY: You're crazy! [Laughed.]

ME: Well, I already have Charlton Heston and President Reagan doing it for free, and I promised Bill Buckley I would see if Tom would also do it for free.

Now I had John's curiosity maxed out.

AGENCY: You have got Heston and Reagan doing a commercial for free? What's the product?

ME: I'm producing a commercial to sell subscriptions to *National Review* magazine, and I read in *TV Guide* that it is Tom's favorite magazine. William F. Buckley is personally waiting to hear what Tom's response is, and I'd hate to go back to him and tell him I couldn't even get past Tom's agent's assistant.

Now John's whole attitude changed.

AGENCY: Maybe I had better put you through to Betty. Just a moment.

A few minutes passed, and then Betty picked up the phone.

AGENCY: This is Betty McCart . . . and John just told me about your conversation. You're not going to believe what I was doing when he came into my office.

ME: What?

AGENCY: I was filling out a subscription card for *National Review*.

ME: You're kidding!

AGENCY: It really is Tom's favorite magazine. He takes it with him wherever he goes. In fact, a few weeks ago we got into a major political argument in a restaurant in Hawaii, and Tom ended the argument by telling me, "Betty, you have no idea what you're talking about. Read this article in *National Review*, and then we'll talk about it." So I read it, and it really did open my eyes to some aspects of the issue that I had never realized before. So here I am, ordering my subscription, when John comes in and tells me about your call.

ME: I can't believe it. Did John tell you that I've already got Charlton Heston doing the majority of the spot, with a cameo appearance by President Reagan? And all I need from Tom is a cameo appearance with a single statement.

My hopes were soaring. Then she burst my bubble.

AGENCY: Steve, I'm sure Tom will be flattered that you and Bill Buckley thought of him, but I can tell you right now, there's no way he'll appear in a commercial.

ME: Are you sure?

AGENCY: Positive! But I should be hearing from him in the next hour, and I'll discuss it with him.

I hung up, deeply disappointed. Why did I ever think I could get him in the first place? After all, only six months earlier I had been told by Betty's assistant that Tom Selleck would not appear in any commercial for any price.
Twenty minutes later my phone rang. It was Betty.

AGENCY: Steve, I really have to apologize.
ME: Why?
AGENCY: Because I was so presumptuous to turn you down on Tom's behalf. It's just that he's always had a flat absolute rule—no commercials! But I just hung up with him, and he wants to do this one!

Needless to say, I was on cloud nine. At the time, Tom was the hottest male TV star in America. As it turned out, Tom, Charlton Heston, and President Reagan all appeared in the commercial. For Charlton and Tom, it was the first commercial they had appeared in since becoming famous. It was also the only nonpolitical commercial in history that included an appearance by a president while in office. The commercial worked phenomenally well. In fact, in the initial rollout, it outpulled any magazine subscription commercial ever produced, including campaigns for *Time, Sports Illustrated,* and *Playboy.* Even William F. Buckley was impressed enough to appear on our corporate film and call us "miracle workers" and the most effective marketing group in America. In fact, Tom's part and President Reagan's part of that commercial can still be seen today, ten years later, in some of *National Review*'s current spots.

Our success with that campaign is not the reason I share this story, but rather to make the first two points of this chapter. First, most of the really good celebrities can't be bought at any price, but they will endorse products they truly believe in. Of the eighty-plus celebrities that have appeared in my productions, many had never been willing to do any commercials whatsoever until we matched them with products they could get excited about. By the way, the *National Review* commercial wasn't the only time celebrities were so enthusiastic about our projects that they gave free endorsements. Ted Danson, Holly Hunter, Larry Hagman, Marion Ross, and Virginia Madsen all gave free endorsements in our Lori Davis infomercials hosted by Cher because they believed in and loved Lori. In that same set of infomercials, Julia Roberts, Arnold Schwarzenegger, Michelle Pfeiffer, Winona Ryder, and Barbara Hershey all gave permission to use their names and photos.

In our case, the vast majority of our celebrity endorsers have been paid for their participation. At first you might think they'd do anything for the money or that they did it only for the money. Both may be true for some athlete endorsers and many "B" and "C" celebrities, but it is never true for an "A" celebrity. For most "A" celebrities, their image and popularity are far more important than making a million or two from a commercial.

For example, when Cher heard that I was producing an infomercial about Lori Davis hair care products, she really wanted to be the spokesperson. "After all," she told me, "I've been Lori's client and number one fan for over eight years, and I've been her guinea pig for nearly every product she's developed!" Lori and I were both thrilled with Cher's enthusiasm and commitment, so we produced Lori's first two infomercials with Cher as the host.

Cher received the same kind of endorsement contract we would give any megastar, so she ended up making a ton of money from the success of the infomercial. Then, after two years of airing the infomercial, she felt her exposure in that and another commercial she had appeared in was hurting her acting career, and she asked us if she could be relieved as the central spokesperson. She added that we could use her in all print advertising and as a voice-over endorser in television and radio commercials. She knew this would result in a much lower income from the project, and yet reducing her TV presence was much more important to her than her income. We understood her concerns and acted accordingly.

To further underscore the money issue, I will tell you that one of the most important parts of my job is recruiting the right celebrity for the right product. Overcoming a financial hurdle in making a deal is not the greatest difficulty I have, it's convincing the celebrity that his or her image and credibility will not be tarnished by an appearance in the commercial. If my company or the product or the way we serve our customers wasn't the absolute best, I couldn't recruit even one "A" celebrity. Not one! So when you see an A celebrity endorsing a product, you can be sure ninety-nine times out of a hundred that the product he or she is endorsing is going to live up to its claims, and the company selling the product is going to back up its warrantees and guarantees 100 percent.

In our earlier days, we occasionally recruited "C" and "B" celebrities because we had not yet built a reputation good enough to attract "A" celebrities. Sometimes even a good reputation and a great product isn't enough to sign an "A" celeb. If it was only a matter of money, these days we could afford to recruit anyone . . . but it's not.

The second point of my Tom Selleck story is my first "insight" for this chapter, which has been the foundational philosophy of my life and my celebrity recruiting efforts:

INSIGHT 1: SHOOT FOR THE MOON. IF YOU MISS, YOU'RE STILL HIGH!

As I mentioned earlier, I had been told by Tom's agency six months earlier that he would never do a commercial for any price, and yet I called his agent with a deal that would pay him no money. Why? Because I knew that if I could get anyone in the whole world to appear in this commercial, Tom Selleck would be the absolute best. So I wanted to start at the top, and then if I got turned down, I'd go for the next best. I always envision the best scenario, and no matter how slim the chances, I always start there. If I miss, I work downward.

Unfortunately, many people do just the opposite. They only shoot at targets they know they can hit. This is a safe way to go, but it nearly always achieves mediocre to below-average results. You'll find that in nearly every personal or business project you undertake, your natural inclination is to set goals you believe you can reach. The only way to break that habit is to ask yourself: If I could achieve anything I want on this project or in this area, what would it be? Then write that down and make it your starting point—and only move downward after you have taken your best shot at the highest target.

When I approached John Ritter in 1987 to be our first spokesman for "Where there's a Will there's an 'A,'" he had just turned down a car commercial that offered him a guaranteed fee of $750,000. I knew that I could offer him a guarantee of only $15,000. He had never appeared in a commercial, and he had turned down an offer from one of America's most prestigious auto makers. No one would have given me a snowball's chance of signing him, yet I made the call to his agent. Why? Because he was at the top of my list for this project. It didn't matter that I had a product nobody had ever heard of or that my guarantee was only one-fiftieth as big as the one he had already turned down. All that mattered was that he was at the top of my list.

Well, to my surprise and overwhelming delight, he listened to my pitch for the product, and because of his concern about education, he decided to do the project. It was tremendously successful, and John ended up making a lot more money than he would ever have made with the car company—but he had no idea what would happen when he started. Once again, belief in the product was a lot more important than the size of the offer.

This strategy of starting at the top and working downward can be applied to any area of life—your job, your outside projects, your relationship with your spouse and children, any area in which you want to see improvement. Wives, if your husband is constantly criticizing you, don't set your sights at reducing his criticism, set your goal one step higher: replacing criticism with praise and encouragement. If you shoot at that goal and miss, you'll still end up with a heck of a lot more than if you merely aimed at reducing his criticism. Instead of your relationship becoming more tolerable, it will become more wonderful.

Just so you know that this philosophy has worked more than once or twice for me in the recruiting of celebrities, I want to show you some of the celebs who have appeared in my commercials and infomercials. Even though many are no longer in the limelight, most appeared when they were at the pinnacle of their careers, starring in their own prime-time TV series or movies or recording successful albums.

CELEBRITY ENDORSERS WHO HAVE APPEARED IN ATC COMMERCIALS AND INFOMERCIALS

Jane Fonda	John Ritter
Cher	Kathie Lee Gifford
Larry Hagman	Frank Gifford
Burt Reynolds	Meredith Baxter Birney
John Tesh	Loretta Swit
Tom Selleck	Michael Learned
Dick Clark	Ali MacGraw
Charlton Heston	Pernell Roberts
Michael Landon	Bob Barker
Harry Morgan	Gavin MacLeod

Dick Van Patten
Merlin Olsen
James Arness
Fred MacMurray
William Christopher
Mason Adams
Pat Boone
Leslie Nielsen
Art Linkletter
Peter Lupas
Senator Sam Ervin
Rosie Grier
Carolyn Jones
General John Eisenhower
Angela Lansbury
Ted Danson
Holly Hunter
Dennis Weaver
Connie Sellecca
Carol Burnett
Robert Wagner
Lindsay Wagner
Teri Garr
Vanna White

Charlie Sheen
Stephanie Powers
Priscilla Presley
Ally Sheedy
Donna Mills
Cathy Lee Crosby
Lisa Hartman
Markie Post
Ed Begley, Jr.
Pamela Bellwood
Ed Marinaro
Glenn Ford
Angie Dickinson
Brian Keith
Tony Randall
Richard Simmons
Peggy Fleming
Robert Reed
Jack LaLanne
Debby Boone
Donna Reed
Lynda Day George
Jerry Lucas

Aiming high when setting your goals is only the first step in achieving higher degrees of success. The second step is equally important. In fact, without it you might as well not even take the first step. It's been a critical part of signing every celebrity I've ever worked with, and it's this chapter's second insight.

INSIGHT 2: PREPARE. DO YOUR HOMEWORK.

Before I meet with celebrities to discuss a deal, I do a lot of homework. I learn as much about them as I can—their likes and dislikes, their desires and fears, their hopes and goals. I find out as much as I can from their agents about them, including their histories and their possible objections or roadblocks to accepting my proposal. Then I design my proposal and focus my presentation on overcoming their obstacles and guiding their minds around any roadblocks. Even though it's impossible to be perfectly prepared, I don't schedule a meeting until I know I have done everything I can to be as prepared as possible. As a result, I go into every meeting believing that I'm going to sign the celebrity. I have never had one celebrity ask one question that I wasn't prepared for. The result is that of all the celebrities I've ever met, I've been turned down by only three, and two of those were on the same project. In those cases, they turned it down because even though they loved the product, they didn't think it was possible to sell it through an infomercial. In the end, they were wrong. The infomercial not only succeeded, it made the celebrities we did sign millions of dollars.

One of the most important parts of preparation is being flexible. For example, you may go into the presentation with a strong preconceived notion as to how you want to accomplish the task, but people often have their own ideas about how *they* would like to achieve the objectives. So you have to be prepared to make mid-course adjustments right on the spot. If you're not flexible, you may miss out on making your idea better, and you might even miss out on the opportunity altogether.

When I meet with a celebrity on a project, I have a preconceived idea as to the format and the theme of a commercial or infomercial. And more often than not, a celebrity has his or her own preconceived ideas that run counter to mine. Instead of immediately dismissing those ideas, I try to blend the best of them into the best of mine. The result is usually a commercial or show that achieves everything I want, while giving the celebrity a theme, format, and script that he or she feels represents his style and fulfills his or her hopes.

The most extreme example of this I can think of happened in 1986 in my first meeting with Richard Simmons. Our company had developed a low-cost exercise device called the Body Styler, which we were going to sell for $19.95 through a two-minute commercial. I had decided I wanted Richard Simmons as the endorser, and his agent arranged for us to meet at Richard's house.

After all the introductions had taken place, I pulled this device out of my briefcase and introduced it to Richard. I demonstrated it and pitched it as hard as I had ever pitched anything. After about twenty minutes, Richard said, "I really like it. I'll pass it around to some of my people, and if they use it and like it as much as I do, I'll do it."

I breathed a sigh of relief, and then Richard surprised me by saying, "Now I'd like to show you something I've been working on." With that he jumped off the sofa, ran into the kitchen, and came back with a plastic bag containing some hand-cut pieces of colored construction paper and a single page of typed instructions. As he handed it to me, I asked, "What is it?"

"It's the easiest and best way to lose weight that's ever been invented, and it ends calorie-counting forever. I call it 'Deal-A-Meal.' He then went on to explain how it worked. My reaction? "Richard, this is without a doubt the most ingenious idea I have ever heard in my entire career. Forget my Body Styler. Let's work on this." The result? We created a whole product line around Deal-A-Meal, and within three months we were airing our first Deal-A-Meal commercial. Since that day we have sold more than $160 million of Deal-A-Meal and Sweatin' to the Oldies products.

What a tragedy it would have been if I had been so focused

on my idea that I had told Richard, "That's a nice idea, but I'm here to recruit you for *my* project, not to figure out how to market yours." We did go on to test the Body Styler with another endorser, and it totally bombed. Had I not entered the meeting prepared to be flexible, we would have shot a commercial with Richard for the Body Styler and might have ended up with a single product and a few million dollars in sales instead of $160 million in Deal-A-Meal sales. By the way, I only launched this project with Richard, and while I was working on it, we did only $10 million in sales. The two people who worked with Richard *after* the first six months and took the sales from $10 million to $160 million were Ed Shipley and Lynn Thoma. Along with Richard and his staff, they created an unbelievable business.

The third step for me in recruiting celebrities is the third step in achieving any goal, and it is one that most people never follow through on:

INSIGHT 3: GO FOR IT.

Many people are able to set their sights high and may even "prepare," but for one reason or another when it comes time to put up or shut up, they find it easier to shut up. If you had previously been turned down by Tom Selleck's agent's assistant and told that Tom would never do any commercial for any price, would you have irritated his agent with a call six months later asking Tom to do a commercial for *free*? If you're like most people, of course you wouldn't. And there was a time that I would have been right there with you. I'm convinced that most people lose their opportunities to achieve success because they never take the shot even when they have a vision of what to aim for.

In her sophomore year in high school, my daughter had the same problem when it came to grades. The last quarter of her freshman year, she pulled in a grade point average of 2.1. It was at that time I met the college professor who had created the seminar Where There's a Will There's an "A." After I received the seminar audiotapes, I handed them to Carol and asked her to listen to them. Here's what she said: "Dad, I'm not an 'A' student, and I never will be. I'm a good athlete and artist, but I don't have what it takes to get good grades."

She was not aiming low, she wasn't even aiming. And if she wasn't aiming, she surely wasn't going to take a shot. I handed her the tapes and said, "Carol, these have literally turned 'D' students into 'A' students. Just for me, please go up and listen to them." She surrendered and somewhat unwillingly went up to her room to listen to them.

A few hours later she came down from her room incredibly excited. "Dad, I'll never get a C or even a B on a term paper again. I'm going to get only A's."

I couldn't believe her enthusiasm or her certainty. "How can you say that?" I asked.

"Because now I know what the teachers want!"

Instantly, she had gone from a student with no target to a student who was not just aiming at the moon, she was ready to start shooting. And shoot she did. Her next quarter she made the honor roll with a 3.4. She made the honor roll every quarter after that until she graduated. In 1994 she graduated from Villanova University with a degree in English and secondary education. My daughter who had never thought she could get good grades is now working on her master's degree. She learned to shoot for the moon, and she learned that once she had her sights set, she had to pull the trigger and go for it!

Last but not least, there's one more critical step that has enabled us to recruit celebrities like no other company in America. It is summarized by the fourth insight in this chapter:

INSIGHT 4: MINIMIZE THE LOSSES. SHARE THE WINNINGS.

We learned this principle with our very first project, and it has guided every deal we have ever made with celebrity endorsers. The strategy has been so effective that it has enabled us to sign up countless celebrities we would otherwise never have been able to recruit. It's not a principle that was born out of genius; rather, it was the only option available to us the first time out.

If you remember our first project, the acne medication, we had only $3,600 available to produce the commercial. At the time Pat Boone was used to receiving endorsement fees of five and six figures. Obviously, there was no way we could afford to pay that kind of fee. We couldn't even afford a fraction of it. In fact, we couldn't afford to pay him anything *up front*. Yet we knew that the only way we could create a successful commercial was to utilize his family's testimonial and his participation as the on-camera endorser.

How do you hire a celebrity as an endorser when you don't have a fraction of what that celebrity is normally paid? The only way you can do it is if the star really believes in the product and believes that you can create a good market for it. In this case we were fortunate that Pat and his family truly believed in the acne medication. We told him that we couldn't pay him anything for the shooting and testing of the spot, but if the test was successful, we would pay him an ongoing royalty on every bottle we sold. He agreed to do the deal. He believed we could successfully market it even though we had absolutely no track record at the time.

As I mentioned in Chapter 4, this turned out to be the incredible success that launched our company. We made a lot of money, and Pat made more than triple the endorsement fees he would have made from any other national commercial—and he deserved every penny.

Hollywood is a very small town, and before we knew it, the top agents were all talking about how much money Pat Boone had made from this project. When I was ready to start making calls to agents to recruit a celebrity endorser for my next project, they not only took my calls, they were eager to talk. And because we had set the precedent with Pat, we were able to convince them that their clients should take a gamble with us and allow us to shoot and test a commercial for a ridiculously low session fee. Our pitch was, "If we get a winner, we will pay them a royalty with no cap or upper limits on earnings." While celebrities didn't relish the thought of shooting a commercial for next to nothing, they loved the idea of making a lot more money than would otherwise be possible.

One by one we started signing "C" and "B" celebrities. At the time there was no way we could sign an "A" celebrity with this kind of deal. But as time went on, "C" and "B" celebrities were making more money with us than "A" celebrities were making with big national advertisers on *conventional* deals. Finally, in 1979, we signed our first "A" celebrity, a movie star with more than two hundred films to his credit: Glenn Ford. The preceding year he had been very successfully used as John Wayne's replacement in a California ad campaign for a bank and as the national spokesperson for Buick.

To our amazement and delight, he agreed to the same kind of deal we had used with all of our "B" and "C" celebrities: a very low session fee and a generous royalty on sales in the event of a national rollout and a successful campaign. The result? He made more from us than he had from his national campaign for Buick and his regional bank campaign combined. He made a lot of money, we made a lot of money, but equally important, Hollywood couldn't believe how much money Glenn was making from a tiny company in King of Prussia, Pennsylvania.

Outsiders and conventional ad agencies criticized us, saying we were paying celebrities a lot more money than they were worth. What they didn't realize was that the celebrities had taken a risk by appearing in the commercial because if it failed, they would net only pennies compared to the dollars Madison Avenue would pay them for a comparable test. Our attitude toward our celebrities from our very first spot was: "Let us test with you for next to nothing. If the spot doesn't work, you've wasted a day of your time and we've wasted the production costs. You won't be getting rich on our loss, but if we get a winner and we make a lot of money, you'll make a lot more with us than you would make from any other commercial campaign."

This philosophy allowed us to minimize our losses, thus allowing us to test more products and commercials. At the same time, whenever we hit a home run, the celebrity ran the bases with us, making it that much easier to sign the next endorser.

Who was right? Us or the advertising and media geniuses who criticized us for "overpaying" our celebrities? Our productivity (profit per employee) is higher than any company in America, and that's *after* paying tens of millions of dollars to our endorsers. Oh, may our competitors continue to be ever so wise.

Notebook for Success
Launching Your Rocket

INSIGHTS FOR SUCCESS (REVIEW)

Insight 1: Shoot for the moon. If you miss, you're still high!
Insight 2: Prepare. Do your homework.
Insight 3: Go for it.
Insight 4: Minimize the losses. Share the winnings.

PERSONAL INVENTORY FOR SUCCESS

1. Using the prioritized list of goals you made at the end of Chapter 2, reconsider them in light of this chapter's first insight. For each goal ask yourself, "Am I shooting for the moon or aiming at the ground?" Now, imagining that you have unlimited abilities and capabilities, aim your sights higher and rewrite each goal to reflect your highest desire in that area.

    For example, if your goal is "fewer fights with my spouse" but your unlimited dream is to have a relationship full of love and happiness, free from all expressions of anger, rewrite your goal to reflect that wish.

2. Looking at the steps you listed for achieving each goal, write down what is necessary to become fully prepared to take that step in the best possible way. Part of your preparation is to think about every conceivable roadblock to taking and completing that step, and then creating a strategy to bypass that roadblock. Once you're prepared to take a step, don't put it off—just take it.

3. In each of your important projects and relationships, how can you better apply the concept of recruiting the help of others in a way that will minimize your losses in the event of failure, and more effectively share the wealth or benefits in the event you succeed?

CHAPTER 9

Getting Rich While Having Fun

If It's Not Fun, You Won't Be <u>That</u> Successful!

"Can You Believe We Get Paid to Do This?"

I have been told that when Steven Spielberg and George Lucas were filming the scene in *Raiders of the Lost Ark* in which Indiana Jones is being dragged underneath a truck while hanging on to his whip for dear life, Steven turned to George with a big grin on his face and said, "Can you believe we get *paid* to do this?" Of course he was saying that this part of his job was so much fun, *he* should be paying for the privilege of doing it, rather than getting paid to do it!

For twenty years I have felt this same way about my job every day I've gone to work. If I was going to dedicate this chapter to anyone, I would have to make three dedications: first, to my partner and best friend since college, Jim Shaughnessy, who taught me how to make every day on the job a "fun" day; second, to my other partners who have provided the environment and incredible friendships that have made it possible to have fun every working day; and finally, to all the wonderful people I've had the privilege of working with over the years—the film crews, the editors and technicians, the artists and vendors, and *most* of the celebrities and actors I have directed. I really can't believe I get paid to do this!

But the purpose of making a job "fun" is not just to increase our pleasure; more important, it is to literally drive our success to unimaginable heights. Most of today's superachievers aren't driven by their desire for money. If they were, Frank Sinatra, Bill Cosby, George Lucas, Steven Spielberg, Bill Gates, and Bunker Hunt (not to mention nearly every other multimillionaire I've ever met) would have quit working years ago. Their jobs, as incredibly hard, demanding, and difficult as they may be, are so much fun, they just can't walk away from them. The same can be said about successful athletes. When Bonnie Blair was interviewed after winning her fifth gold medal in speed skating, she said, "I was just having fun, doing what I love to do." The reverse is also true. When most successful athletes retire, their usual comment is, "It's just not fun anymore."

One world-renowned motivator for whom I have tremendous respect once said, "Don't complain to me that you don't like your job because it's such hard work. Of course it's work. If it *wasn't* work, they wouldn't call it 'work.'" His goal was to criticize *complaining* about work, but he gave the impression that work is supposed to be "hard" not "fun." I'm convinced that in order for work to be rewarding, it has to be both hard *and* fun. When it is, it's better than just about any other activity in life.

**INSIGHT 1: IF IT'S NOT FUN, YOU PROBABLY WON'T SUC-
CEED.**

Most of the people I have met in my life would never describe their job as fun. And consequently, most of the people I
have met will never get rich! When a job isn't fun, you approach it with a host of attitudes that can stifle and even suffo-
cate any tendency toward success. These attitudes can create
insurmountable hurdles to "super" success or achievement.
They can range from the extreme of hating or dreading work to
simply "showing up and doing my time." When you think of it
that way, it's not much different from prison—or at least it has
the *attitude* of prisoners.

Not having fun on the job not only prevents achieving "super success" in your career, it usually prevents "super success"
at home and in most other areas of life. After all, we spend the
majority of our waking hours on the job. We start the job when
our energy level is at its highest and leave the job when the majority of our energy has been drained. If we come home with
less energy and somewhat unhappy, to a spouse and children
who usually desire and need more attention and energy than
we have to give, we tend to withdraw, creating both tension and
frustration in our family relationships.

It doesn't have to be this way! No matter how miserable you
are on your current job, there are steps you can take to make it
a lot more enjoyable. The more enjoyable it becomes, the more
successful you'll become. And the more successful you become
on your current job, the better chance you'll have for moving to
higher success levels with your current employer or with future
employers. And when you're happy and successful on the job,
you come home with a much more upbeat attitude and a
higher energy level.

All this to say that the answer isn't to quit your current job
and find one that's more fun but rather to make your current
job more fun. And as you achieve more success in that job,

even better opportunities for more success will begin to appear.

"How the heck can I make such a miserable job *fun*?" This may be your first reaction. Obviously some jobs are a lot harder to make enjoyable than others. Being a roofer in Phoenix in August or a gas station attendant in Minnesota in January is not my idea of a fun job. And you can't turn an ordinary rock into a diamond. I would never be so naive or insensitive as to imply that any job can be turned into a delightful cosmic experience. However, there are steps you can take that will make any job more enjoyable. Even an ordinary rock that is tumbled and polished by a capable craftsman can be turned into something beautiful. If you have a dead-end job or a job that's the pits, making it more enjoyable will most likely be the key to moving out of that job into a more satisfying and rewarding one.

How do I draw that conclusion? Simple. The more you learn to enjoy your job and the people you work with, the more successful you'll become. And the more successful you become, the more likely you'll advance in your company. The more you advance in your company, the more desirable you'll be to other companies. Simply stated, enjoying your job breeds success, and success breeds upward mobility.

Jim Shaughnessy has been my best friend since college. During that time I have seen Jim in an array of jobs, ranging from physical labor to teaching junior high, to sales, to his current position with our company of overseeing our manufacturing needs. No matter what job he's been in, no matter who he's worked for, no matter how hard his circumstances or how vicious his adversaries, he has always had fun in every single job. The fact that he's made every job fun doesn't mean he hasn't worked hard. To the contrary. I'm convinced that, for nearly everyone, the more you enjoy your work, the harder you work. And the less you enjoy your work, the more you avoid working hard.

The amazing thing is that even though you work a lot harder when you enjoy your work, it doesn't *feel* like you're working harder. In fact, when you really enjoy your work, it doesn't feel like work at all. Michael Landon was one of the hardest workers I've ever known. I once told him that I worried about the kind of hours he was keeping and how hard he was working. I said, "Mike, it's got to be taking its toll. You've got to be feeling the stress." He answered, "Steve, I'm having so much fun, I don't even feel like I'm working. I don't feel stressed out at all. In fact, look who's talking. Look at the schedule you keep." I had to give him the same answer he gave me: My work never feels like work. Mike was not only one of the hardest workers I've ever known, he also had more fun on the job than anyone I've ever known.

What are the keys to making work or a job more fun? There are three general factors that need to be dealt with to make any job more fun. One relates to your attitude, one relates to the people you interface with, and one relates to the work itself. (If you're thinking, "Oh, great. The only thing worse than my job are the idiots I have to work with," don't worry, you can still have fun on the job—if you make that choice.)

The first and most important element in raising the "fun factor" or "enjoyment factor" of your job is changing or adjusting your own attitude. Is your attitude toward your work and the people you work with positive or negative? How often do you find yourself complaining to yourself or others about your work? Do you complain about your boss, your work, your fellow workers, your subordinates, your clients, or your suppliers? Do you wake up in the morning dreading your work and end your day with a "can't wait to get out of this place" feeling?

Law of Negativity: The more negative you are about your work and the people you work with, the less likely it is that you will become successful.

It's an absolute law that the height of the hurdles to your success is in direct proportion to the degree of negative feelings you have about your work. The more negative you are, the higher the hurdles become. If your reaction is, "How can I have a positive feeling about my work or the idiots I work for or with?" then I have news for you. The bad news is that as long as this is your attitude, your chances of increasing your success are next to zero. Get ready for a long, disappointing, and frustrating career.

Law of Attitudes: You alone are responsible for your attitudes, and you alone can make them more positive.

The good news is that no matter how negative you are toward your work and the people you work with, you can convert your attitudes from negative ones to positive ones. It's a lot easier than you think, and you don't have to wait for your work or the people you work with to change.

Do you see the incredible good news about this statement? Most of us think that our feelings and attitudes are controlled by how others treat us and by how hard or bad our jobs are. That simply is not true. If you say, "But you don't know my boss" or "You have no idea how hard my work is," my reply is, "That just doesn't matter." How can I say that? Because I know that adversity isn't our enemy, adversity is our friend. Adversity is the strongest force in our lives. It deepens our character and increases our creativity—if we let it! If we resent it, we become angry, bitter, and contentious. If we realize it can be our ally, it teaches us endurance, patience, persistence, and tenacity. And if we welcome it as a friend, it can result in tremendous creativity that acts as a booster rocket to success.

So the first element in making your job more fun and enjoyable is changing or adjusting your attitude to make it more positive.

The second element in making your job more fun and enjoyable is building enjoyable relationships with the people you work with. This includes the people in your company, those above you, those beside you, and those below you; and the people you interface with outside of your company, your customers, your vendors, suppliers or contractors, and your other outside contacts. Improved relationships don't just happen, they have to be developed and nurtured. That requires time and attention, even if only a little. Strategies and Tips at the end of this chapter gives you some steps you can take to significantly improve your relationships on the job.

The third and final element in raising the fun factor is learning to "strive to excel." Striving to excel isn't just an ethereal principle, it's a specific attitude that manifests itself through clear-cut actions you can take as part of your daily work routine.

There are five actions in striving to excel:

1. Dream or visualize.
2. Convert the dream into goals.
3. Convert your goals into tasks.
4. Convert your tasks into steps.
5. Take your first step, and then the next.

It sounds easy. It is easy. The Notebook for Success at the end of Chapter 2 takes you through this process. If you want to be really successful, while you are learning to implement these "dream" to "step" actions, help those you work with to do the same to achieve *their* goals.

INSIGHT 2: ANY OTHER WAY OF GETTING RICH IS A WASTE OF LIFE.

I'm sure that there are plenty of moderately successful people and even a few super-successful people who achieve their success *without* having fun. What a waste! I have read about family members in family-owned businesses struggling for power and hating one another. So what if they're successful! What good is success if you're miserable or if you make others miserable? My ex-boss who got a charge out of firing and humiliating me achieved a fair measure of success in his career. But at the end of his career when he looks back at his own success, I'm sure he'll realize how empty it was and how fleeting the satisfaction was that he derived from it. The joy of my success isn't just what I have right now, it's looking back at all the fun times I've had with the people who have been successful with me.

When I shoot a commercial or show, I spend tens of thousands of dollars a day—dollars out of my pocket and the pockets of my partners—so I'm very aware of what's happening every minute. Every extra hour I take costs us thousands of dollars. I'm also aware that every extra hour we work, the celebrity becomes more tired, loses more energy, and has a much harder time performing at his or her best. With these factors in mind, a shoot day is never a leisurely stroll. There's an enormous amount of pressure to get the absolute best out of the cast and crew and to do it as quickly as possible. But even in this high-pressure, high-cost situation, I am still faced with a choice: Make the day fun, or make it hell!

Because I have the budget to surround myself with the best crews in Hollywood, I don't have to put directorial pressure on them to get them to do their jobs capably and quickly. Because they are so professional, they do that automatically. The same is true with the actors and actresses I work with. So when things are running behind schedule, instead of climbing all over them and creating more tension, I tend to try to lighten things up. The result is, they enjoy their work all the more, and instead of giving me 80 percent they give me 110 percent. We get more done in less time. At the end of the day, even though we may be exhausted, we're happy and we're proud of what we've accomplished.

It is not uncommon for a celebrity to take an hour or two more than planned in makeup and wardrobe. That starts our on-camera work late, and it backs up the meal break for sixty crew members and usually pushes us into overtime in the evening. And yet, rather than trying to put pressure on the celebrity to hustle up, I usually try to relax him or her and tell the celebrity to take all the time that is needed. Why? Because I want that person to enjoy the day rather than feel the stress of it. Because after all these years, I know that if the celebrity enjoys the day, it will show in the performance in front of the camera. And that will make the difference between a great-looking show and a mediocre one. The celebrity's attitude in front of the camera is a lot more important than an "on-time" lunch or the bucks I would save if we wrapped on time.

By the way, I have known plenty of successful people who have stopped having fun after they've become successful. This metamorphosis can take years, or it can happen almost overnight. Some of our companies are created around people who had never had any significant financial success before we entered their lives. One person had been trying to sell his product for years, all to no avail. When I negotiated his contract I asked what kind of money he would like to make. His answer was, "I drive a Toyota . . . does that tell you?" I asked him if he would be happy if he made $100,000 a year, and he replied he'd be thrilled. Within a few months we were paying him $10,000 a month. Was he thrilled? Not even close. Only a month after we began airing the show in which he was featured, he complained to two of our employees, "If they think I'm bustin' my butt for ten thousand a month, they've got another think coming." Overnight, the success had gone to his head big time!

But for every bad story I have a hundred great ones. Stars

such as Michael Landon, Kathie Lee and Frank Gifford, Tom Selleck, and Harry Morgan (M*A*S*H's "Colonel Potter") not only have a lot of fun themselves but also make work fun for everyone they work with. Instead of treating crews like servants, they treat them like buddies. Hollywood has lots of spoiled brats, but it also has some of the nicest and most considerate people I've ever had the pleasure to meet. And all but a small few of the eighty-plus celebrities I've worked with have made my work a blast. And for those who have been a pain in the butt (and you know who you are), all I can say is, you've made my work with the nice ones that much sweeter.

So if you're miserable in your current job, the good news is that you don't have to be! You can take the necessary steps to make it a lot more enjoyable. If you're waiting for success to happen or simply *hoping* that you'll enjoy your job more or get a more enjoyable one, let me tell you it usually doesn't happen that way. You have to take the initiative, and if you do, both the fun and the success will follow.

STRATEGIES AND TIPS FOR BUILDING MORE ENJOYABLE RELATIONSHIPS

1. Realize that every single person you encounter during your day wants to be noticed, appreciated, and treated like a friend instead of simply used to perform a service. For example, when you place a call to someone in another company (or at your company) and a secretary answers the phone, don't just ask for the person you're calling for, take at least a moment to acknowledge the secretary by name. Ask how her day is going and so forth.

2. Take the initiative to be thoughtful at times when it is not expected. Write a note, give a word of encouragement, ask a question about the family, or do any of a hundred things you can do to show you care—and do it some-

times when it's not expected or when there's no discernible reason to do it.

3. Take a personal interest in the other person's desires, dreams, and goals. Let the person see that you're genuinely interested in his or her success and happiness.

4. Never criticize without sandwiching the criticism between two slices of praise or encouragement. Start with encouraging words and end with encouraging words. Remember, the person probably feels worse about the mistake, failing, and inadequacy than you do. Criticism is constructive only when it leaves the other person motivated to want to improve. If the person is deeply hurt by the way the criticism is delivered, he or she will be totally *demotivated*. The person must sense that your goal in criticizing is for his or her future benefit and improvement—not merely to express your anger or frustration.

5. Spend more time listening than talking . . . and listen *first*. Everybody needs to be heard, so everybody appreciates a listener.

6. Order Gary Smalley's video series "Hidden Keys to Loving Relationships." In my opinion it is the best material on building great relationships ever recorded on videotape. You can order his tapes by calling 1(800) 982-6750. (I hate it when authors recommend something but don't tell you where to get it.)

Notebook for Success
Making It Fun

INSIGHTS FOR SUCCESS (REVIEW)

Insight 1: If it's not fun, you probably won't succeed.
Insight 2: Any other way of getting rich is a waste of life.

Laws for Achieving Success

Law of Negativity: The more negative you are about your work
   and the people you work with, the less likely it is that you
   will become successful.
Law of Attitudes: You alone are responsible for your attitudes,
   and you alone can make them more positive.

PERSONAL INVENTORY FOR SUCCESS

1. How negative are you? On a scale of one to ten—ten being the most positive, zero being the most negative, and
   five being neutral—rate how negative or positive you are
   in the following areas:
   A. Feelings about your work
   B. Feelings about the people you work with:
      Your superiors
      Your fellow workers
      Your subordinates
      Your clients, vendors, outside contacts

2. Are you willing to become more positive in the areas you
   rated below a ten in question one above?
   If yes, you will become more successful.
   If no, you probably are about as successful as you'll ever be.

3. On a scale of one to ten, how much fun is your job? (Ten is a blast every day; five is moderately enjoyable; and one is hell on earth.)

4. List the things you enjoy most about your job and the things you dislike the most.

5. List the people you relate to on your job, starting with the ones you relate to most often and ending with the ones you relate to the least often.

6. Next to each name on your list, rate how you relate to them. (Ten is a great relationship, you enjoy them and they enjoy you; five is a mediocre relationship; zero is no relationship; minus ten means you can't stand being around them.)

7. Having read Strategies and Tips for Building More Enjoyable Relationships, write down ideas that you can implement to show each person that you value him or her. You can use these to increase your enjoyment of the relationship. Start with the names at the top of your list.

CHAPTER 10

Creative Alternatives

The Secret to Turning Roadblocks into Springboards

From the brink of disaster to the launching pad of success: Left in the lurch by an unscrupulous company, the self-centered jumped ship while the committed survived, and broke the bonds of gravity.

Almost no success story follows a path straight up like a rocket ship. Instead, the trajectory is usually more like a mountain range that has gradual rises and also plateaus. In our case, we even had a couple of major downslopes along the way. One of them was so drastic, in fact, that it nearly put us out of business. This near-fatal event came from the life insurance side of our business. As I mentioned earlier, in 1978 we were the first company to sell life insurance directly to the consumer successfully through television, but because we did not own an insurance company, we ended up working with the National Liberty Corporation (NLC).

We used our commercials to generate inquiries that we sold to National Liberty. They in turn mailed out direct-mail conversion kits that explained the policies in detail and provided an insurance application to the inquirer. Even though this arrangement made us a significant profit, another insurance company came to us and offered what seemed to be a much better deal. Instead of buying leads from us, they would give us half of all the profits generated from each insurance policy we sold, for the life of the policy. We would use our commercials and TV time to generate an inquiry and would be responsible for creating and mailing the conversion kits. According to the insurance company, this system would generate a long-term income stream that would dwarf the amount of money we were making from selling leads.

To help us with the conversion part of this process, we recruited a manager from NLC. We offered him a piece of our company, which he quickly accepted. But when he thought about the risk of leaving a secure job, he backed out. When he backed out, four of the partners said "good riddance," but Bob and I persisted in talking the rest into going forward to try to change his mind. After much coaxing, he again reversed his decision. Looking back, I think we should have yielded to the majority. Anyone who is offered an entrepreneurial position and is afraid to accept it should turn and run. And equally true, those offering the position to him ought to do likewise. We thought we were gaining a brilliant partner who knew an area of the business we did not and who would be grateful for the opportunity to stand on the launching pad and board a rocket about to take off. As you will see, that was not the case.

With our new man on board, we were ready to begin this insurance project. Our first commercial featured a life insurance plan for veterans, and General John Eisenhower (Ike's son) was our first spokesperson. During the next five years we generated tens of millions of dollars in insurance premiums, blowing away all our competitors. In addition to General Eisenhower, we created successful campaigns with Glenn Ford, Michael Landon,

Dick Van Patten, Harry Morgan, Bob Barker, and Merlin Olsen. Although we were able to receive a portion of the profits we were generating, most of the residual profit was left in the insurance company. It was our belief that one day we would be able to take our half of the tens of millions of dollars in profit we were generating out of the insurance company by selling them our half of the business.

Then in 1985 when we thought we were riding the rocket ship into outer space, we discovered it was pointed toward earth. The insurance company was sold to outside investors, and we decided that it was time to cash in on our half of the business. We had been told that our half was worth $20 to $25 million. But a few months after informing the new owners we wanted to cash in, we were told that our half was worthless and that they were not even going to pay us the $4.5 million they owed us for the TV campaign we had just run. Not only did they owe us, we in turn owed that amount to our suppliers.

The new owners of the insurance company weren't afraid of our suing them because they knew that we could not last the time it takes to fight, win, and collect on a lawsuit. They also threatened not to free us from an exclusive marketing contract we had with them. We had no choice, so we swallowed hard and signed a separation agreement, walking away from the millions of dollars they owed us.

We had no money, we had no campaign, we had no new products. All we had was $4.5 million in debt we couldn't pay. It looked as if we were doomed to collapse. Here's what happened.

INSIGHT 1: NOTHING IS BETTER THAN A GREAT PARTNER.

First, the president of the insurance company liked us a lot more than he liked the new owners, so he quit his job and asked if we'd like a new partner to help us get hooked up with another insurance company. We had nothing to lose and Ben Weaver had very little to gain, but he talked our bank into extending their deadline for the repayment of our bank debt of approximately $2 million. How did he do that? He and his wife pledged all their assets (which took them a lifetime to earn) to cover the loan. If we went down the tubes, our new partner would go down with us, losing everything he owned. But that's not all he did. He set out to find an insurance company with which we could enter a joint venture. In a matter of weeks he had found a new company and had cut a great deal for us.

A short time later Bob Marsh and John Marsh began working out terms with all our suppliers to postpone the payment of our debts. Dave Marsh worked out arrangements with the television stations to accept a slower payment schedule and to continue to extend us credit. And Ed Shipley and I worked our butts off to develop a new campaign for the new insurance venture. We were all working against the clock, and if we failed, we would all lose everything we owned, including our homes. One of our suppliers, the owner of the telephone answering service we used, not only allowed us to postpone the repayment of the $250,000 we owed him, he also wrote us a check for $1 million and said, "It's yours at no interest, and if you guys go down the shoots, don't worry, I'll be okay."

Another one of our suppliers told us to take whatever time we needed to pay what we owed him and offered to lend us $50,000, saying the same thing. Years of treating our suppliers like princes instead of like slaves was now paying off beyond anything we could ever have expected.

We signed our agreement with the new insurance company in mid-November. Two weeks later I was having dinner with Harry Morgan. I told Harry about our predicament, and since we now had a new insurance company, I needed to create a new campaign that would generate enough profit to save our company. Harry said, "I'll be your endorser if you like." It was a very nice offer, but I explained to Harry that since I had used him as an endorser a few years ago, I could not use him now because his "pulling power" with our consumers was "used up."

But Harry persisted. His wife of forty-seven years had died two years earlier, and Harry and I had become close friends. He had been totally devastated by the loss of his best friend and the mother of his four sons. I felt it was very nice of him to make the offer, but I knew it wouldn't work. Then Harry said something that caught my attention. "Steve, you know how hard it's been on me to lose Eileen. And if I had had financial problems on top of the emotional devastation, I wouldn't have been able to go on. Well, I didn't have financial problems, but a lot of widows do. I can't imagine the agony they go through, but I'm willing to talk about what I've been through."

I told Harry I could never ask him to do that, and he replied that he knew I could write it in a sensitive enough way that he could do it. Six days later we shot the commercial; a week after that we tested it, and a week after that we rolled it out. We had gone from concept to national rollout in six weeks, a process that normally took our competitors nine to eighteen months to complete. In three months that campaign generated a $3 million profit, leaving us only $1.5 million in the hole. But the hole was still potentially deep enough to put us out of business.

INSIGHT 2: NOTHING IS WORSE THAN A BAD PARTNER.

Ben Weaver and the original partners were doing everything they could to keep the company alive, but the partner who had been coaxed on board six years earlier was a whole different story. He was concerned only about himself. He was constantly asking, "What's going to happen to *me?*" never *us*. Even worse, he was continually bad-mouthing the other partners behind their backs. In fact, he had even called some of us "totally incompetent" to our suppliers. But that wasn't *all* he was doing.

He was secretly negotiating a deal to join one of our competitors and take his knowledge of our business and our future marketing plans with him. One day he walked into our morning staff meeting and sternly announced he was leaving and joining one of our competitors. With that, he turned and walked out of the office.

We were all in shock. He had been treated like one of the family. Bob Marsh had given him the opportunity of a lifetime—literally every major break in his career. And now when the going had gotten tough, he not only was jumping ship, he was also going into competition and taking our competitive secrets with him. He had told our attorney that we didn't have a prayer of surviving, and as far as he was concerned, "T.D.I.O. The dream is over!"

So now we were not only trying to keep the ship afloat but our own former partner was launching torpedoes in our direction. Then came the campaign that finally took us out of harm's way.

I signed Gavin MacLeod (captain of the *Love Boat*) to do our next insurance campaign. It was a life insurance policy for people over fifty, and they couldn't be turned down for the coverage regardless of their health. Even though I had a good spokesman, I didn't have a hook for the commercial. I was telling my dad about it when he suggested that I use his testimonial. He had gone through three heart surgeries and could no longer buy life insurance, but he was able to get this coverage.

I wrote two commercials, one with Gavin MacLeod by himself and one with him and my mom and dad. The one with my mom and dad was the winner, the big winner. It generated the highest response (in terms of weekly in-bound calls) of any direct-response television commercial in history. Over 125,000 calls per week! That campaign generated enough profit to pay off our remaining debt and put us ahead of the game. Once again, thanks, Mom and Dad!

Meanwhile, our ex-partner created a commercial that was

almost identical to the one with my mom and dad except that it used a different celebrity (the one I had been planning to recruit next) and a different elderly couple. But his campaign generated only a small fraction of the business ours did, and the company he had joined was soon out of business. His dream was over. Ours was about to take off!

INSIGHT 3: THE DREAM IS NEVER OVER!

For those who are truly committed to a vision, the dream is never over until the dreamer is dead. The Bible says that "where there is no vision, the people perish." When we give up on a vision, even though we may not perish physically, our soul—our drive and our spirit—can be mortally wounded. Our ex-partner's dream was to make millions of dollars. When we were sinking, that dream was over for him, and he jumped ship to try to save himself. He had no real love or commitment to the rest of us. From the very beginning he was in it only for himself. Our dream was very different. Yes, we wanted to make millions, but that wasn't why we were staying together. We were staying together because we loved *what* we did, and we loved *who* we were doing it with! None of us wanted to work in any other business, and, more important, none of us wanted to give up working with one another.

INSIGHT 4: DON'T GIVE UP SO EASILY. GET BUSY AND GET CREATIVE!

Very few people are fortunate enough to see all of their dreams fulfilled or all of their goals realized. When a dream seems to be dying, it's so easy to throw in the towel, and that's exactly what most of us do. Most people in our society want gratification, success, and fulfillment of their dream exactly as they dream it and exactly when they want it. So when the dream starts to fall apart or fails to materialize within our time constraints, we quickly abandon it. This is true in both business as well as in relationships.

Where are the qualities of determination, perseverance, responsibility and loyalty, faith and commitment, ingenuity and creativity? People who see their dreams fulfilled rarely do so because of luck. They realize their dreams because they put everything they have into achieving them. They draw on all those qualities from within their hearts and minds.

If you don't have a reservoir of these character qualities to draw on, most likely your dreams will die easily. Not all of our dreams come true. We take a lot of swings, and we strike out just like anyone else who comes up to the plate. But we keep dreaming. As Thomas Edison said, "When the going gets tough, the tough get going!"

When a dream isn't coming true or a goal isn't being realized, rather than quickly abandoning it, get busy and get creative. Don't be afraid to make mid-course corrections, revising your goals. If you encounter a ten-foot wall, instead of giving up because "there's no way I can jump ten feet," get busy and get creative. Look for a little lumber and build a twelve-foot ladder. Then climb over the ten-foot wall, one foot at a time. A professor of entrepreneurship at UCLA was recently asked, "What do successful entrepreneurs have in common?" Her answer was, "Tremendous tenacity. They don't give up."

My first two commercials with Richard Simmons selling his "Deal-A-Meal" product generated about $10 million in sales. My third commercial bombed, and it looked as if we had squeezed all the juice out of that orange. I had all but given up on the project but didn't feel that bad because $10 million in sales wasn't a bad number. Even though I thought that that dream was over, my partner Ed Shipley didn't agree and simply revised it. Instead of selling Deal-A-Meal with a two-minute commercial, he would try to sell it with a thirty-minute infomercial, as we were doing with "Where There's a Will There's an 'A.'" The result? Deal-A-Meal got an extra six years of life and additional sales of over $160 million. Can you imagine if Ed had followed my lead and accepted my assessment? Thanks, Ed!

INSIGHT 5: NEVER RACE A THREE-LEGGED HORSE.

So when *do* you give up on a dream? Bob Marsh tells the story of the time he had a meeting with David J. Mahoney, the former CEO of Norton Simon Industries. When he walked into Mahoney's office, he noticed a statue of a three-legged horse on his desk. When Bob asked why he kept a "broken" statue on his desk, he replied, "To remind me never to race a three-legged horse." In other words, there *is* a time to recognize that an idea is a bad idea or a dream cannot be fulfilled. There *is* a time to give up and move on to a new horse. Some people have such a deep emotional attachment to their ideas or goals that they never give up. They hang on to a "bad dream" until it pulls them under and they drown.

Every direct-response project has a life cycle. Some live for six months, some for six years. There did come a time when two infomercials in a row didn't generate enough orders on Deal-A-Meal to keep it on the air. After winning $160 million in prize money, *that* horse couldn't win any more races. So we took Deal-A-Meal off the air and put it into retail stores.

Without a doubt one of the hardest choices for any individual, manager or entrepreneur, is to recognize when the dream has turned into a three-legged horse and to take it out of the the race. One of America's leading consumer goods companies recently spent more than $2 million on an infomercial to launch a new product line around a particular celebrity spokesperson. It was their first attempt to sell their products via an infomercial.

They put it on the air, and it bombed beyond belief. We heard that for each $1,000 spent in broadcast time, it generated only $50 in sales. If that is true, it's the worst pulling infomercial we've ever heard of. It's not a three-legged horse, it's more like a horse with *no* legs. And yet to our amazement we heard that the company created a new infomercial on the same product with the same spokesperson. Needless to say, the money they spent on that one went right down the toilet. Too bad the owner of that company never met David Mahoney and saw his three-legged horse!

We recently produced a beautiful infomercial on a world-renowned product line. Our spokesperson was the star of one of America's top ten prime-time television series. We had a great product, a wonderful spokesperson, and a breathtakingly beautiful infomercial. We put it on the air, and even though it was profitable, it wasn't nearly as profitable as our other programs. We even tested a lower price, and it didn't do any better. Rather than spend millions more trying to improve the results, we realized we had misjudged the size of the market for this particular product and relegated it to a secondary role in our media plan. Throwing in the towel on any project is just as hard for us as it is for anyone else, but we do it! And then we move on to the next dream and the next project.

Throw everything you have at your dreams and goals, but when it becomes obvious that one of them is a horse with three legs, put it out to pasture and focus your time and efforts on finding a new one.

How do you know when the dream is over or when it only needs to be revised? Most people usually give up too quickly, so in my opinion it's better to go the extra mile before giving up. It's better to err on the side of trying too hard than on giving up too quickly. Nine times out of ten you shouldn't give up. Get busy and get creative. But just be ready for that occasional horse that has only three legs. When you find one, don't try to turn it into a racehorse. One of the big advantages of having great partners is that even if one of us can't see that the horse has only three legs, we have six other pairs of eyes—and more often than not, at least in our case, the *majority* is usually right.

Notebook for Success
Developing Your Creative Alternatives

INSIGHTS FOR SUCCESS (REVIEW)

Insight 1: Nothing is better than a great partner.
Insight 2: Nothing is worse than a bad partner.
Insight 3: The dream is never over!
Insight 4: Don't give up so easily. Get busy and get creative.
Insight 5: Never race a three-legged horse.

PERSONAL INVENTORY FOR SUCCESS

1. Review Strategies and Tips for Identifying and Recruiting Mentors at the end of Chapter 4.
2. Make a list of former goals and projects (business or personal) that you gave up on before they were fulfilled or completed.
3. Next to each goal or project you gave up on, write down the reason you gave it up. Then rate each one with GUTE (gave up too early) or 3LH (three-legged horse).
4. If you have any GUTEs, list what you think it would have taken to turn it into a successfully fulfilled goal or completed project. What needs did you lack that could have been met by the right kind of partner (such as financial, marketing, administrative, and so forth)? Write them down next to each GUTE.
5. Look at your prioritized list of goals and projects from Chapter 2 and write down the specific hurdles that could prevent you from successfully fulfilling those goals and completing the projects.
6. List any creative alternatives you can think of that might help you over those hurdles.

7. Write down the kind of qualities or talents you would choose in a partner to help you overcome those hurdles.

8. Are any of your current goals or projects potentially a three-legged horse? If so, what event or set of circumstances would it take for you to *know* it's a three-legged horse that should be pulled out of the race and retired?

CHAPTER 11

Billion-Dollar Steps to Instant Selling and Persuading

How to Sell Something in Two Minutes That Most Salesmen Need Hours to Sell

After more than eight hundred two-minute commercials and 20 million responses, selling everything from insurance to books, from videos to cosmetics, even an idiot can learn what works and what doesn't.

One of the first statistics I learned at my first job was that even a good life insurance agent usually needed three appointments of about two hours each to sell a policy to a new client. So when Bob Marsh had the idea of using two-minute commercials to sell life insurance policies, I didn't share his enthusiasm. The year was 1978, and even though my two-minute commercials were selling millions of dollars' worth of products, the thought of achieving the same kind of numbers selling a service like life insurance seemed impossible.

A two-minute commercial gives you only a hundred seconds of sell time because you have to leave twenty seconds to give the consumer the telephone number and address. How can you hope to sell a life insurance policy in one hundred seconds of sell time? Bob had the answer: Use the commercial to give the viewer the basic information needed to make a decision to request a free information kit instead of trying to use the commercial to actually make the sale. That plan sounded a little easier, but the best mail-order insurance companies in America had tried that concept years ago and had failed.

Bob's other idea turned a single into a grand slam: recruit a celebrity endorser who has so much credibility that you don't have to waste any time in the commercial establishing the credibility of the company or its insurance policy. If you can gain that much credibility from the mere presence of the endorser, you can spend the entire one hundred seconds talking about the problem and the way this insurance policy solves the problem. And maybe, just maybe, enough consumers will respond to make the commercial a winner.

Our target market was adults over fifty. We recruited Senator Sam Ervin, who had headed the Watergate Investigating Committee hearings on TV just a few years before. His integrity was above reproach, and he had gained the respect of tens of millions of older Americans. How credible was he? When we walked through Los Angeles International Airport, men and women stopped in their tracks, set down their luggage, and started applauding. I had never seen anything like that with any other celebrity I had spent time with.

As it turned out, Bob's two ideas were right, and we produced a winner for us and our insurance partner. We also began a new era in life insurance sales. By the time we jumped out of the TV insurance business in 1987, the market had become saturated with large life insurance companies trying to duplicate what we had accomplished. In our first eleven years, I wrote and produced approximately eight hundred two-minute television commercials, which generated tens of millions of dollars in insurance premiums and more than $100 million in product sales. And to my amazement, other than our insurance business, no other company ever succeeded in knocking off our products. (A knockoff is a product or a campaign that someone produces as an imitation of someone else's product or campaign.) In a country where just about anything successful is copied or counterfeited, the fact that we haven't been successfully copied is somewhat of a surprise.

I think there are several reasons. First, no one (other than insurance companies) ever figured out how successful our campaigns were. (As a private company, we made none of our sales figures public.) Second, industry experts and trade publications kept saying that celebrity endorsers didn't increase sales and were therefore an unjustifiable expense. Third, and most important, TV mail order is an extremely specialized field, and only a very small number of people understand how to make it work.

Successful TV marketing is like crossing a very narrow footbridge without any handrails over a very deep canyon in a fog so thick you can't see two feet to the left or right. Companies who have never tried to cross it come running onto the bridge thinking it is as wide as a Los Angeles freeway.

I remember that one of America's leading long-distance telephone companies came up with a TV direct-response campaign to put subscribers on a special monthly program. They figured that each subscriber they generated would spend about $200 per year in long-distance fees. If they could generate one subscriber for every $50 they spent on TV time, they would make a nice profit. So their ad agency produced a series of beautiful, very expensive commercials. Of course they didn't use a celebrity because everyone knew that it would be a waste of money to do so. And instead of producing two-minute spots, they produced thirty-second spots. The phone company was very excited about the commercials until the national campaign began to air. The response was terrible. The media cost per order was $15,000. In other words, they generated only one order for every $15,000 they spent on TV time—$200 in sales for every $15,000 in advertising. Talk about falling off a bridge into the Grand Canyon!

So how do we hit grand slams while America's corporate giants strike out? Before I give you the answers, let me give you an analogy. Without a doubt, Michael Jordan is considered by many to be the greatest basketball player ever to play in the NBA. Does that mean he can cross town to Wrigley Field and become the next Ted Williams or Willie Mays? He found out the hard way that different sports require radically different talents. But imagine if instead of walking to Wrigley Field, he caught a cab to Chicago's O'Hare Airport and climbed into the cockpit of a 747 and told the crew to sit back and relax while he flew the plane to New York. He has no previous experience in the cockpit, no training as a pilot, no knowledge of navigation—but don't worry, he's a superstar on the court. Would you stay on that plane or find the nearest exit?

Equally ridiculous is the notion that because a company is a Fortune 500 company it can enter TV direct-response marketing with no experience, no training, no knowledge of what kinds of commercials work, no knowledge of what times of day and which TV stations work, not to mention what copy approaches, pricing decisions, and celebrity endorsers work and which ones don't. There are hundreds of variables, any one of which can result in failure.

Is there a foolproof formula for creating a successful TV direct-response campaign? No! But even though I don't have a foolproof formula, I *do* have a set of navigational charts. A formula is rigid, and when correctly applied, it always produces the same results. That being the case, there is no formula for our business. But we do have a set of guidelines, charts that we have created as we have navigated the oceans of our industry for twenty years. Through a history that has taken more than eight hundred commercials and scores of national campaigns to produce, running in various time periods on nearly every television station and cable superstation in America, we have charted where the currents run, where the reefs and sandbars lie, and, most important, where the best harbors are located and the most efficient ways to get to them.

To create a successful TV direct-response campaign, there are ten different areas in which critical decisions must be made:

1. Product selection
2. Endorser selection
3. Offer decisions
4. Copy strategies
5. Precise scripting
6. Media strategy and selection
7. Upgrade offers
8. Telephone scripting
9. Fulfillment decisions
10. "Bounce-backs" and back-end marketing (going back to customers at a later date with additional marketing offers, either through the mail or outbound telemarketing)

In this chapter we're going to look at one page from the charts, namely, the key elements that I have used in creating successful two-minute scripts that have sold tens of millions of dollars' worth of products. We'll look at some of the other charts in the next chapter.

The key elements I use to sell a product in one hundred seconds of TV time can be used to make any sales pitch and salesman a lot more effective. Equally important, they can be used to effectively persuade anyone, at home or at work.

INSIGHTS FOR MAKING RECORD SALES IN RECORD TIME!

INSIGHT 1: GRAB ATTENTION.

Imagine that you're watching your favorite program on television. When the program breaks for a commercial, what do you do? Tell everyone else in the room to be quiet so you can listen more intently? Hardly! Much more likely, you reach for the remote to either turn down the volume or switch stations—or you get up and leave the room to get a snack, go to the bathroom, or whatever. So how on earth can I sell you anything in the next two minutes? Sound impossible? It is! Unless I can instantly grab your attention and hold it for at least five seconds. Therefore, the first important element in making any sale is grabbing the attention of the potential buyer.

You may think that this element is not relevant to you because you work with your clients face to face. *Au contraire!* Whether you are making a sales presentation to a potential client or a new client, or whether you're pitching an idea to your boss or to your spouse, you still have to "grab" the person's undivided attention in a way that will enable him or her to really "hear" what you're saying and remember it. Whoever you're addressing has his own problems, ideas, and thoughts competing for his attention at the exact moment you're trying to acquire it! If you assume that you have his undivided attention or that the person is really "hearing" what you're saying just because he is standing a few feet away, looking at you, you don't understand the human mind or personality.

So how do you grab someone's attention and lock it in to what you are about to say? In commercials, I have found three ways that work the best. The first way isn't applicable to you personally, though the second and third are. The first and best way to grab attention is to use a well-known, well-liked celebrity spokesperson who isn't doing other commercials. Why is this so effective? If you were at a party and all of a sudden you heard the voice of a friend you haven't seen for a long time, where does your attention turn? Right to her! At that same party, if a major celebrity walked in, what would happen? Everyone at the party would instantly focus in the direction of the celebrity and start sneaking peeks.

The same is true on television. The right celebrity immediately grabs the attention of the viewer, and I have found absolutely nothing that works better. But there are two other ways to grab a viewer's attention that also work wonderfully. The most effective is to ask a question; the other way is to make a surprising or strong statement. While you probably can't get a celebrity to come along on your sales calls, you can start your presentation with a good question or a surprising or strong statement.

Our company was launched with the opening statement of my first commercial: "Acne is painful both physically and emotionally. I don't care if you're a teenager or an adult, acne causes embarrassment and anxiety." I can promise you that all those who had acne or had a child with acne, when they heard Pat Boone make that statement, their attention was instantly "grabbed" and locked in. Cher opened our first infomercial introducing the Lori Davis Hair Care Line with "Did you ever look at your hair and want to cry?" Cher's mere presence was a hook in itself. Having her ask this question was icing on the cake. Every woman has looked in the mirror at her hair and wanted to cry at least once in her life. By asking this question, Cher had not only locked in viewer attention, she had thrown away the key! The result was the fastest-growing hair care line in history!

INSIGHT 2: SALT YOUR COMMUNICATION.

You have heard the adage, "You can lead a horse to water, but you can't make him drink." That's simply not true! You can make the horse drink every time! All you have to do is salt his oats when you feed him. He'll be more anxious for a drink than you are after a bowl of salty popcorn. In communicating, whether orally or in writing, there is a way we can salt our words that will make the audience incredibly thirsty to hear or read more. And if you keep salting your communication, you can keep that audience glued to every word you say until you have said everything you want to say.

So what's the salt? Before I tell you what it is, let me tell you that it always works—whether you're talking to a child, speaking to a group, writing a commercial directed at the masses, or talking to the CEO of General Motors. I have never used this principle even once when it failed to captivate the attention of whomever I was addressing. It is without a doubt one of the two most powerful communication tools I have ever discovered.

In fact, I've been using it on you for the last three paragraphs, and especially the last two. Salting simply means creating a significant amount of curiosity about the information you're going to communicate *before* you communicate it. In this instance, I "salted" you by telling you about the benefits and effectiveness of a principle before I revealed its definition, and you hung on every word. I may have lost your attention at various times during this book, but I'm sure you didn't close this book at any time during the last three paragraphs.

Let me give you another illustration. One of our products is a video series on relationships that features Dr. Gary Smalley, a marriage and family counselor. Gary is the absolute best when it comes to practical advice on building better relationships, and he's also one of the most effective communicators I've ever known. He has written thirteen consecutive best-sellers and has had as many as one hundred thousand men attend a single session on relationships.

In our infomercial featuring John Tesh and Connie Selleca, here are a few of the "salting statements" Gary made:

"Did you know that there are two things you women do to men that make us want to run away from you? I know you don't mean to do it—and you certainly don't realize how much we hate it—but when you do it, we can't get away from you fast enough."

After Gary explained what those two things were, he then salted his audience again with the next statement: "Every man has one particular need—which happens to be our greatest need—and when you meet that need, we want to get a lot closer to you, we want more time with you. But when you don't meet that need, if someone else does, we'll be drawn to that person—and no, it's *not* sex!"

How many women in our audience do you think changed channels during those two statements? *Not one!* As you can see, salting your communication holds the attention of your audience, whether it's one individual or a million viewers. One important rule about salting: If you sense that you do not have the undivided attention of your listener or that he's not anxious to hear what you're saying, add even more salt before you finally get to your point.

In the example above, if Gary didn't have the women sitting on the edges of their seats after his first dose of salt, he would just add another one: "In fact, when a wife consistently fails to meet this one need, the chances of her husband having an affair skyrocket—because if the need goes unmet long enough, he'll start seeking someone else to meet it. It's that strong a need!"

If Gary senses that the hearers are now desperate to learn the need, he reveals it. And when he reveals it after the right amount of salt, they drink it in and never forget it.

INSIGHT 3: USE EMOTIONAL WORD PICTURES.

This is the single most powerful communication technique ever used in communication, whether written or oral. Its purpose is not to grab or retain a person's attention but rather to stimulate the right side of the hearer's brain so that he or she can actually feel what is being said instead of just hearing it. Why? Because when you feel what someone else is saying, you never forget it. History's best communicators were masters at incorporating emotional word pictures (EWPs) into their speech and writings. Simply stated, an emotional word picture is a statement or story that enables the hearer to visualize what is being said. It can be as short as a single word or as long as a two- or three-minute story. Because I think this technique is so powerful, I've included a further explanation of EWPs in Strategies and Tips for Powerful Communication at the end of this chapter.

In an earlier chapter I said that your goal should be to make your subordinates' goals and success one of your priorities, and if you do, you'll ride on top of their rocket ship to new heights of success. That picture communicated a very simple but often overlooked truth: that the more successful your subordinates become, the more successful you'll become. The picture of riding on someone else's rocket ship locks that concept into your mind much more effectively than simply saying, "If you make your subordinates successful, their success will make you more successful."

Gary Smalley tells of an employee who used an emotional word picture with his boss that resulted in an immediate pay raise and a promotion to a preferred shift, changes he had been passed over for a week earlier in favor of another employee. John (the employee) knew that Tom (his boss) was a highly decorated World War II veteran whose memories of his combat days were still a source of deep emotion. John took his time to create an emotional word picture that would use Tom's memory of combat to enable him to understand and feel what John was feeling. Here's what he said:

"Tom, do you remember when you were in the infantry who your best friend was in your platoon?"

"Sure. It was Pete Harris."

"Well, imagine you and Pete are in the trenches right before the battle starts, and Pete tells you, 'Tom, if I could have any soldier in the world fighting alongside of me, it would be you. You're the best.' And then, right after he says that, he points his rifle at you and shoots you right in the thigh. Then he says to you again, 'Tom, you're the best. It'll always be you and me,' and then *boom,* he shoots your other leg. And he continues, 'Tom, when this battle starts, I'm not going to let anyone hit you. I'll take the hit before I let that happen to you,' and then *boom,* he shoots you in the arm. How would you feel?"

His boss answered, "Are you kidding? I'd be devastated."

"Well, that's exactly what you've done to me, and that's exactly how I feel."

With that, his boss asked, "What on earth have I done, and what can I do to fix it?"

He then told his boss, "For the last year you have told me over and over again how much you appreciate me, that you never want to lose me, and that nobody works as hard as I do. But last week when the promotion opened up on the morning shift, you passed right over me and gave the job and the raise to Barry. You shot me in both legs and my right arm, and I'm totally demoralized because the shots didn't come from an enemy, they came from the one person I respect the most around here."

John's boss was visibly concerned, and he replied, "I had no idea I had hurt you like that. You've got the raise as of today, and you'll start on the morning shift on Monday."

Nothing communicates a feeling better than an emotional word picture when it is created and used *correctly!* Strategies and Tips for Powerful Communication gives you a step-by-step guide based on Gary Smalley's material that will enable you to use EWPs effectively in both your personal and business communication.

WHAT'S MY SYSTEM?

When people hear what our track record is, they always ask, "What's your formula?" Not being a complicated person, I do not have a complicated formula. I've already revealed a big part of it in Chapters 6 and 7 and with the first three insights of this chapter: *The foundation is laid before the writing begins!*

My system begins with an attitude, an attitude of respect for the potential buyer. Nothing in my commercials will insult the buyer's intelligence. No screaming. No singers floating around in a toilet. No stupid questions. The buyer is not only as smart I am, he or she is probably more sensitive and better able to see right through anything that is phony, insincere, or condescending. Therefore, anything I write will be extremely logical and will play to the buyer's intelligence rather than insult it.

I must understand who my potential buyer is and what need or desire my product will fulfill. If I have a product that doesn't legitimately play to a genuine need or desire, trying to fabricate a need or desire greatly increases the probability of a strikeout and radically decreases the chances of hitting a home run. I must understand what specific surface need my product fulfills and, equally important, what underlying or foundational needs and desires I will be appealing to.

For example, in trying to sell a woman a new makeup base, the surface need or desire is to have a complexion that looks flawless without looking overly made up. The underlying desire is to look naturally more beautiful. And the underlying need is to be more visually appealing to others, more confident and less self-conscious about her appearance.

When selling an organizing notebook, I appealed to the surface need to be organized. The underlying needs were to achieve more in a limited amount of time and the fulfillment of knowing that specific things were accomplished each day.

I must understand why my product fulfills the buyer's needs or desires better than any other product on the market. If your product doesn't have at least one competitive edge that you really believe in, you have a problem when it comes to selling it—whether you're trying to sell it through a commercial or a sales presentation.

Treadmills have been around for a long time. Motorized treadmills range in price from $300 to $6,500. When Jane Fonda's company first told me about a non-motorized treadmill they had developed that would sell for between $300 and $400, it sounded like a pretty tough sell. After all, who would want to buy a non-motorized treadmill when a motorized one is just a few bucks more?

Then two things happened that turned me around. First, I read in a consumer magazine that buying a motorized treadmill for less than $1,100 was a waste of money because the cheaper models were vastly inferior. Second, I saw Jane Fonda's prototype demonstrated. I was blown away. I realized that it had some major advantages over the "cheap" motorized treadmills. It even had some incredible advantages over the expensive $6,500 models! Advantages such as simplicity, portability, safety, controllability, and built-in music, to name a few. So when it came time to write an infomercial about it, I focused on these advantages and made such a strong case that we had a lot of buyers purchase ours even though they already owned expensive motorized ones!

I make a list and prioritize every possible objection and excuse a potential buyer could use for not purchasing my product. Even though you may have the best product in the world that fulfills the needs and desires of every buyer better than any other product on the market, they will still have plenty of reasons not to buy your product. You need to know what those reasons are and how strong each one is.

Going back to Jane Fonda's treadmill, as I thought of the objections and excuses for not buying, I came up with two lists: one of the factors that keep my potential buyers from starting and sticking to any exercise program, and one of the specific objections that might keep them from making a purchase of this particular piece of equipment. Here are the two lists.

Exercise Blockers

1. No fun—don't like exercise
2. Takes too much time
3. Not convenient
4. Too expensive to go to health club
5. Home equipment is too expensive
6. Afraid of doing something wrong—injuries
7. Don't know what kind or how much exercise to do
8. Never succeeded in sticking with it before

Reasons for Not Buying This Treadmill

1. I can buy a motorized treadmill for just a little bit more.
2. I can buy a cheaper non-motorized one from a catalogue or shopping channel.
3. A different type of equipment might be better (skier, stair climber, rower, or cycle).
4. I'm not an expert. I don't know which type of equipment is best.
5. What if I get it and don't like it?
6. It's too expensive. I can't afford $360.

I make a list and prioritize how the product overcomes each potential objection or excuse for not buying the product. This is

the most critical part of the preparation before scripting a written or verbal sales presentation. To follow through on my example of the treadmill, I listed each of the objections and excuses for not exercising or buying this equipment, followed by the answer I came up with to overcome that objection or excuse.

BLOCKER 1: **No fun—don't like exercise**
ANSWER: The built-in cassette player lets you listen to music and walk to the beat, making your workout a lot more fun. Also, because there's no noisy motor, you can watch TV while you're working out.

BLOCKER 2: **Takes too much time**
ANSWER: A new Stanford study shows that you gain the same benefit from three ten-minute workouts that you get from one thirty-minute workout, so you don't have to carve out large blocks of time. Also, because the unit is in your home, you don't have to waste time getting to and from a health club. Finally, the fact that the unit has a permanent incline and no motor (you provide the power), you get a more intense workout in less time!

BLOCKER 3: **Not convenient**
ANSWER: Because this unit is kept in your home and you need to use it for only ten minutes at a time, this equipment makes exercising very convenient.

BLOCKER 4: **Too expensive to go to health club**
ANSWER: With this equipment you won't have to go to an expensive health club.

BLOCKER 5: **Home equipment is too expensive**
ANSWER: This treadmill is a fraction of the price of quality mo-

torized treadmills, and a twelve-payment plan makes it affordable for everyone!

BLOCKER 6: **Afraid of doing something wrong—injuries**
ANSWER: You have been walking all your life. Using this treadmill is as easy as walking up a hill. And because the belt starts when you start and stops when you stop, there's no possibility of injuring yourself by stepping onto or off a moving belt. It's the most user-friendly piece of exercise equipment on the market. Also, the accompanying video and "Jane's Walk to the Music" audiocassette make sure you go at the pace that's just right for you.

BLOCKER 7: **Don't know what kind or how much exercise to do**
ANSWER: The accompanying video will show you how to determine what pace to keep and how long to keep it. The audio cassette has workouts for beginners, intermediate exercisers, and advanced exercisers.

BLOCKER 8: **Never succeeded in sticking with it before**
ANSWER: The ease, convenience, and speed of progress will give you everything you need to stick with this program.

And then there are the responses to the reasons for not buying this treadmill:

REASON 1: **I can buy a motorized treadmill for just a little bit more.**
RESPONSE: According to *Consumer Reports, quality* motorized treadmills range in price from $1,100 to $6,500. That's three to twenty times as expensive as this one. Also, a motorized treadmill has many disadvantages, such as maintenance, safety, weight, not being portable or "storable," being complicated and intimidating.

REASON 2: **I can buy a cheaper non-motorized one from a catalogue or shopping channel.**

RESPONSE: The technical breakthrough on this unit is a patented horizontal flywheel not available on any other non-motorized treadmills. So the belt moves smoothly with your stride, and at the same time, once it's moving, it doesn't run away from you as cheaper units can.

REASON 3: **A different type of equipment might be better (skier, stair climber, rower, or cycle).**

RESPONSE: These all give a good aerobic workout, but the learning curve is tougher and the potential for injury is greater. Also, none of these are portable and storable. You've worked hard to decorate your home—do you want an ugly, bulky piece of fitness equipment in the middle of a room?

REASON 4: **I'm not an expert. I don't know which type of equipment is best.**

RESPONSE: That's why I (Jane) have two experts here to tell you why they prefer this piece of equipment over any other piece of equipment on the market today.

REASON 5: **What if I get it and don't like it?**

RESPONSE: It comes with a full money-back guarantee. If you don't like it for any reason whatsoever, you can return it for a full refund.

REASON 6: **It's too expensive. I can't afford $360.**

RESPONSE: Our twelve-payment plan of $29.95 per month makes it affordable for everyone.

As you can see, listing and answering potential objections and excuses provides the critical foundation for creating an effective presentation.

Law of Preparation: You cannot create nearly as effective a sales presentation without the proper foundational preparation as you can with the proper foundational preparation.

SCRIPTING YOUR PRESENTATION

Having now created a prioritized list of all the objections and excuses for not buying your product or service and your answers to each of those objections and excuses, you are now ready for the final stage of preparing a written, verbal, taped, or filmed presentation. In your case the presentation may be a thirty-minute sales call. In my case the presentation is a two-minute commercial, a thirty-minute infomercial, or a single- or multipage print ad. Regardless of what form your final presentation takes, the above lists give you the guts of the content of your presentation.

When you are scripting your presentation, you need to include seven critical steps.

1. *Instantly* grab the listener's or viewer's attention with as strong a hook as you can create.
2. Once you have the undivided attention of your buyer, set up the problem or problems your product is going to solve.
3. Salt the presentation with curiosity-building statements or questions as often as necessary to keep the buyer's undivided attention.
4. Using emotional word pictures to make your most important points crystal clear and unforgettable, utilize your product benefit list and your responses to objections and excuses to form the body of your presentation.
5. Use testimonials of satisfied customers, industry experts,

or other credible sources to substantiate the credibility of your product and your claims.

6. Use comparisons to other products and prices to build a perceived value of the product that far exceeds the selling price of the product.

7. Close the presentation with a quick summary (when time allows), a risk/reward comparison, and a clear-cut reason for action.

In the Appendix for this book I have included my two-minute commercial script and my thirty-minute infomercial script featuring Jane Fonda selling our "Walk to the Music Fitness Tread." These will enable you to see how the critical elements are scripted into final form. By the way, the Jane Fonda infomercial turned out to be the most successful infomercial in TV history. It became the most successful mail-order campaign in American history, with sales passing the $145 million mark in its first five months. As you can see, my system works.

STRATEGIES AND TIPS FOR POWERFUL COMMUNICATION

The following material is my condensation of Gary Smalley's principles for creating word pictures. It is taken by permission from the manual of his video series Hidden Keys to Loving Relationships.

Definition of a Word Picture: A word, statement, or story that creates an instant picture in the hearer's or reader's mind that clarifies what you're trying to say and communicates a feeling that you want the hearer to experience or identify with.

Five reasons to use word pictures:

1. They grab and direct a person's attention.

2. They have the power to change a person's thinking, be-
   liefs, and life.
3. They make communication "alive."
4. They lock words into a person's memory.
5. They provide the gateway to deeper relationships.

Five steps to creating and using an emotional word picture:

1. Set aside specific time to create an effective word picture.
   Occasionally you might be able to create a good one
   spontaneously, and as you become skilled at creating and
   using word pictures, you'll be able to create some in a few
   seconds and others in a few minutes. In the beginning,
   however, it could take you ten to twenty minutes to do it
   right when you're trying to communicate something very
   important.
2. Learn about interests of the people with whom you want
   to communicate. Get to know their hobbies, their likes
   and dislikes; how they spend their spare time; who their
   favorite singer, actor, or athelete is; their most treasured
   memories; what makes good days good and bad days
   bad; and so on.
3. Create your word picture from one of five inexhaustible
   sources: Their interests, their past or present, everyday
   objects, nature, and imaginary stories.
4. Practice using the word picture, first by yourself and then
   (if appropriate) on a friend.
5. Pick a convenient time with minimal distractions to communicate your word picture.

Notebook for Success
Persuasion Techniques Worth a Billion

INSIGHTS FOR SUCCESS (REVIEW)

Insight 1: Grab attention.
Insight 2: Salt your communication.
Insight 3: Use emotional word pictures.

Laws for Achieving Success

Law of Preparation: You cannot create nearly as effective a sales presentation without the proper foundational preparation as you can *with* the proper foundational preparation.

PERSONAL INVENTORY FOR SUCCESS

Do not limit the use of the insights and formulas I give in this chapter to your sales presentations. They can be used effectively to communicate your ideas for anything and to persuade your hearer or reader to take the specific action. These ideas can be used to illuminate and persuade a spouse to do those things you consider important, whether it's attending a meeting with you that he or she normally avoids, redecorating a room, going on a vacation, or buying a new car. You can use these insights to sell your ideas to your boss, your subordinates, or your peers.

The more you use these techniques, the more skilled you'll become in using them and the more effective they will become in serving your goals.

Make sure everything you say in your presentation treats your listener with respect and avoids condescension. Use the following concepts to create a written sales presentation of one of your existing products or of something you want to persuade someone to do:

1. Describe your listeners and list their desires or needs that your product or idea will fulfill.
2. State why your product fulfills these needs or desires better than any other product or idea available to the listener.
3. List and prioritize every possible objection and excuse your listener might use for not purchasing your product or accepting your idea or proposal.
4. List and prioritize how your product or idea overcomes each objection or excuse.
5. Script a sales presentation that uses the following techniques.
   a. Create an opening that will immediately "Grab the listener's or viewer's attention" with as strong of a hook as you can create.
   b. Set up the problems your product or idea is going to solve.
   c. Salt the presentation with curiosity-building statements or questions as often as you need to keep the buyer's undivided attention.
   d. With emotional word pictures to make your most important points crystal clear and unforgettable, use your product benefit list and your responses to objections and excuses to form the body of your presentation.
   e. Use testimonials of satisfied customers, industry experts, or other sources to increase the credibility of your product and your claims.
   f. Use comparisons to other products and prices to build a perceived value of the product that far exceeds your selling price of the product.
   g. Close the presentation with a quick summary (when time allows), a risk/reward comparison, and, finally, a clear-cut call to action.

CHAPTER 12

Maximizing Minutes and Multiplying Resources

Building Businesses Instead of Selling Products

Sell a product that people use once, and you can make millions. Sell a product that people use every day, and you can make hundreds of millions.

INSIGHT 1: YOU HAVE ONLY SO MUCH TIME. ALLOCATE IT WISELY.

In December 1987 I wrote and produced my first successful infomercial, "Will Your Kids Make the Grade?" It sold a two-tape video set called "Where There's a Will, There's an 'A,'" and John Ritter was the celebrity endorser. Our company was close to going under when the show was produced. Had it failed, there's a good chance we would have sunk with the show. Fortunately, it took off like a Patriot missile, and we went along for the ride.

When the show first tested, we were all astounded by the response. The partners figured that if we could run it nationally for four weeks without the response falling apart, we would make $100,000 each, which was half of what we normally made in a year. Our company chant quickly became "Four More Weeks!" After a whole year of "Four More Weeks," with each partner earning over $1 million, our chant changed to "Four More Years!" We got our four years with this product, along with $160 million in sales and millions in profits. Not bad for a self-help educational video that never made it to a single retail shelf!

But the success didn't stop with "Where There's a Will There's an 'A.'" In 1988 my partner Ed Shipley produced his first infomercial. He took our simple Deal-A-Meal product that featured Richard Simmons and turned it into a package including a cookbook and an aerobic video entitled "Sweatin' to the Oldies." Like "Where There's a Will, There's an 'A,'" the response was phenomenal. As I mentioned earlier, to date we've done over $160 million in sales with this product line, too.

Then in 1989 our company made a decision and a commitment that turned out to be another milestone in our business. It started with a meeting with a makeup artist, Victoria Jackson, in December 1988. That night she showed me a cream foundation she had created that seemed so sheer, you couldn't even tell if she was wearing any makeup at all, and yet it made her skin look flawless. She called it The No Makeup Makeup. Although I was extremely impressed with the product, I knew we couldn't make an infomercial profitable by selling a single product for only $19.95.

Victoria had had the product for more than five years and had never been able to market it successfully. She had been turned down by every cosmetic company she had approached, with the exception of one network marketing company. They gave her a contract but went out of business before they could do anything with the product. She had even been turned down by me four years earlier when she was the makeup artist on one of my shoots. She had tried to interest me in the foundation, but I saw the perceived value as too low to sell in even a two-minute format.

All of this to say that this time I was really impressed with the product, but once again the perceived value and the price were too low for our kind of marketing. I then asked her the question that was to change the course of our business: "If we provided the money for research and development, would you be able to create an entire line of makeup?" She said she was already working on a color line, and could easily develop the rest. I asked what items we could include, and the price each one would sell for in a department store. We made our list, and the total perceived value of all the items we equaled $230. Now we were talking!

The next few months were spent creating the items we had talked about, writing the infomercial, and preparing the "bounce-back" brochures that we hoped would keep our customers buying the product once they were satisfied with their initial purchase. In June 1989 we tested the infomercial that featured Ali MacGraw and Lisa Hartman. It had good-news/bad-news results. The good news was that it generated a very successful response. The bad news was that to manufacture enough inventory to fulfill our orders would cost us more than $10 million. If we bought all that inventory and for some reason the national rollout didn't produce the same results the test did, we could be out of business overnight.

What would you have done? You have a good business that is making you over $1 million per year. If you successfully launch a new, ongoing cosmetics company, you will add to that income. If you launch it and it doesn't succeed, you could lose everything—your current income, your home, your job, your entire business. We decided to take the risk because the potential reward was too great, and we went on the air nationally in October 1989. The result? Overnight, Victoria Jackson Cosmetics became the fastest-growing cosmetic company in history. From our first week on the air, our sales topped $1 million per week. By comparison, it took Mary Kay Cosmetics, one of the largest cosmetic companies in America, nearly fifteen years to reach that kind of weekly sales volume.

For the first twelve weeks it looked as if we were riding a rocket ship to the moon. Then came the bad news. It turned out that our credit card authorization rate (credit card orders approved by the credit card company) was significantly lower than we had anticipated, our cost of goods was a little higher than we had anticipated, and our order-taking costs and customer service costs were also a little higher than we anticipated. Added together, that all spelled trouble—*big* trouble. Our nice profit margin (the difference between our sales price and our costs) had shrunk to almost nothing. It looked as if we were only a few weeks away from losing money on every order we were taking. If that turned out to be true, we would have gambled our business and lost!

In our panic to save that project and our business in general, John Marsh asked me to come up with a continuity program we could offer our customers. (A continuity program is one in which customers can enroll in a club to receive automatic shipments of product every so often, in this case every three months, and return it if not pleased.) I quickly wrote a script for our telemarketing operators in which they would try to enroll our customers in Victoria's Beauty Club. Within a week we were testing it at our outbound telemarketing service. To our relief, one out of every three customers was willing to sign up because she liked our product so much. The result was that we could afford to run the infomercial, selling product at breakeven (not making money but not losing money), knowing that we would make our profit on customer reorders and on our continuity orders.

For customers who weren't willing to enroll in our beauty

club, we created catalogues that we mailed to them twice a year. It took us nearly three years of investment and deficit spending before we started making a significant profit. After three years and a $30 million investment, we finally started making a profit on our customer base. If we never spend another dime generating new customers, that satisfied customer base will create millions of dollars of profit per year for many years to come. We had discovered a simple but wonderful principle: It's better to build a business than simply sell a product. Even after our infomercials had been off the air for three years, that base kept producing tens of millions of dollars in annual sales because we had built a solid customer base and kept coming out with new products. We finally went back on the air with a new approach in May 1995, and our sales are now greater than ever.

It sounds like an obvious concept, and yet very few of our competitors do it. They still focus on selling products. Why? The answer is just as simple: It takes a lot more time, money, and risk to invest in or build a business, and most of our competitors aren't willing to make that kind of commitment or take that kind of risk. To date, our Victoria Jackson Cosmetics company has generated nearly $250 million in sales, with over half of that in the form of reorders and continuity orders. Had we not come up with a viable continuity program and other back-end marketing programs such as our catalogues, we would have been out of the cosmetics business by our thirteenth week and probably out of business altogether.

Why is it so much smarter to use your efforts to build an on-going business instead of just selling a product? The answer is that all of us have limited resources. Time, money, and managerial capabilities are all limited resources. I have eight to ten hours a day to work, five days a week. That's all I have. Given the choice of investing that time to make a sale or create a business, the wisest use of my time is to create a business. The same is true of money. The amount of cash and credit available to invest is limited, so if I can use it to create a business instead of just making a sale, that becomes the best use of our money.

Since creating Victoria Jackson Cosmetics, we have used our infomercials to create other businesses, including America's fastest growing hair care line (Lori Davis Hair Care); Cher Beauty Products; Westgate Fitness (Jane Fonda Treadmill); and various video companies. We currently have nine projects in development, with seven of them involving potential ongoing businesses and only two involving individual product sales.

If you are a business owner or manager, you probably see what I am talking about here: You should dedicate those limited resources to building an ongoing business centered on long-term relationships with satisfied customers. But what if you're not in any kind of position to build businesses? The underlying philosophy is just as relevant to you. It's relevant to both your business life *and* your personal life. Use your limited resources (time, money, creativity, and physical and mental energy) to achieve lasting, ongoing, long-term results rather than merely completing a task or achieving a one-time goal.

APPLYING THIS BUSINESS PRINCIPLE TO YOUR PERSONAL LIFE

On the personal side, for example, instead of focusing your attention and efforts on getting your mate to do something *you* want to do, focus your efforts on learning your mate's ongoing needs and desires and learning what you can do to fulfill those needs and desires on a long-term basis. Gary Smalley says one of the greatest needs of a woman is to feel safe and secure in a relationship, and one of the greatest needs of a man is to feel admired. Gary points out that even though these are tremendous needs that often mean the difference between a fulfilling relationship and a divorce, most women and men don't feel their needs are being fulfilled.

Applying the principle of building businesses rather than selling products to this primary need of a wife would mean that rather than focusing on trying to get your wife to do what you want to do, you change your focus to building her security and safety factor. You become a better listener, actively communicate and demonstrate your love for her, reduce your criticism, and end any stated or implied threats of abandonment.

If you're a woman, you would be able to focus on what you can do to indicate your honor and admiration for your husband. If you tell me, "But you don't know my husband. There's nothing to admire about him," let me give you an example from the first video in the series *Hidden Keys to Loving Relationships*. Gary Smalley lifts up an old beaten-up violin. Its bridge is broken and is dangling by its strings. Gary asks the audience how much they think the violin is worth, and everyone laughs. Like everyone in the audience, you think $10 or $20. He then reads the inscription inside the violin: "1723, Antonin Stradivarius." Everyone in the audience gasps. What looked like a worthless piece of junk is now an object of tremendous honor, one with a worth over $800,000. As Gary passes it around to people in the first row, they handle it gently, with respect. Has anything about the violin changed? Not at all. The only difference is that it is now perceived differently; instead of being viewed as a piece of junk, it is now viewed as a rare treasure.

We can choose to honor and admire anyone or anything we want. No matter how junky someone may seem, when we look closely enough, we can find attributes that are worthy of praise and honor. The only catch is that we have to *choose* or *decide* to honor that person. The principle of working to build instead of simply to persuade or sell applies to all personal relationships as well. For instance, when a couple focuses on saying and doing things that honor, respect, and admire each other, their own personal self-worth begins to skyrocket.

This same principle can be applied just as easily to any job. If your focus is simply to do what's expected or required of you, you will receive only what you expect to receive, which is the minimum amount of pay, respect, and achievement your job can give. If, on the other hand, you view your job as a business that you can build, you will focus on building relationships and productivity, which will result in long-term growth and achievement.

> *Law of Limited Resources:* Good *use of limited resources is the most effective enemy of the* best *use of limited resources. Don't substitute good for the best simply because it's easier, cheaper, or faster.*

At first my partners were a little worried about my writing this book and the potential help it would be to our competitors by sharing concepts such as this one. After thinking about it, however, we agreed that sharing these concepts wouldn't help them that much because most of these concepts involve swimming upstream, and most of our competitors usually choose to go with the flow. It's cheaper, easier, faster, and safer. Unfortunately, over the long term it's also a lot less profitable. And that brings me to the next insight.

INSIGHT 2: DON'T BE CHEAP!

It's a lot easier to be cheap than not. Most businessmen I know tend to be cheap in particular areas of the business where they shouldn't be. Until recently, for instance, most of our competitors spent less than $100,000 per infomercial while we were spending many times that amount. With an industry success rate of less than one out of two hundred, I guess they figure that the less they spend, the less they'll lose. They were not only cheap in their production budgets, they were cheap in the areas of product development, product quality, and customer service. The result? Lots of one-time sales but little or no profit. When they recruited celebrities, instead of spending big bucks to recruit a major celebrity, they'd spend small bucks to hire a minor celebrity. The result? Minor sales and profits. By the way, in recent years a few of our competitors have changed direction, taking the high road instead of the low road, and I salute them.

Remember the lesson of Chapter 6: "That woman in the supermarket isn't an idiot." Your buyers must be treated with respect, and that means giving them quality products with real value and presenting those products in a quality way—not in a way that insults their intelligence. The question should never be "How much do I have to spend to make the sale?" but rather "What's the best quality I can give the consumers at a price they can afford?" Then spend as much as you need to deliver that quality at that price.

Also, if your goal is to build a business, don't be stingy with your vendors, suppliers, employees, or sales reps. Don't be extravagant or foolish, either. Be fair. If they're good, show them how much you appreciate them—where it counts. One company I worked for treated most suppliers as if they were slaves. The company tried to beat the suppliers down on pricing, make next to impossible demands on delivery and service, and all the time let them know who was the client and who was the supplier. When American Telecast went into competition with this particular company, we used many of the same suppliers and vendors. Instead of treating them like servants, we treated them like family. Instead of trying to beat every last cent out of them, we focused on paying a fair price for their goods and services. Instead of letting them always buy our lunches, we took *them* to lunch. The result? They bent over backward trying to give us the best products at the best prices in the shortest amount of time possible. If we were under a deadline and our competitor was under a deadline, guess who got first priority?

It may pay to be cheap in the short run, but in the long run, being considerate and fair goes a lot further. Some of these suppliers were the ones who saved our business when we nearly lost everything. The adage "You get what you pay for" is true. Even truer is "It's not just *what* you pay, it's *how* you pay." You can pay someone the same amount with a sneer or with a smile, and the reaction you get will be totally different. Our suppliers always felt *appreciated* by us and *used* by our competitor. So while you should be fair with your payment, you should be generous with your appreciation.

Notebook for Success

Removing the Limits of Your Limited Resources

INSIGHTS FOR SUCCESS (REVIEW)

Insight 1: You have only so much time. Allocate it wisely.
Insight 2: Don't Be Cheap!

Laws for Achieving Success

Law of Limited Resources: *Good* use of limited resources is the most effective enemy of the *best* use of limited resources. Don't substitute good for the best simply because it's easier, cheaper, or faster.

PERSONAL INVENTORY FOR SUCCESS

How do you spend your limited resources?
1. On a plain sheet of notebook paper, guesstimate how you spend the 168 hours of your average week. Draw seven vertical lines across the paper (Sunday through Saturday). A standard 8½ x 11 sheet of paper has more than enough horizontal lines to handle 24 hours. Write the times down the left-hand margin, starting with the time you usually get out of bed, and proceed to label all 24 hours.
2. For each day, in *general* terms, fill in the time blocks with how you *think* you spend your time. If your job is fairly routine five days a week, you can just fill in each hour of Monday and run arrows in that time period across through Friday. If, on the other hand, every weekday is different (you're in the office on some days, out of the office on some; take half-hour lunches some days, and hour lunches on others), you'll need to fill in each block each day. If you currently use a day planner, then you can sim-

ply look at the last week or two and be very accurate as to how you spend your hours.

3. After you've completed the above exercise, make a second sheet but don't put anything in the hour boxes. Keep the second sheet with you throughout the next week, and fill and record in a word or two how you spend each hour.

4. After one week of keeping an accurate record on the second sheet, compare the second sheet with the first one. You're likely to be amazed at the difference between how you thought you spent your time and how you really spend your time. More important, this simple exercise will make you much more aware of each hour of your day. Our time is very precious and usually our most wasted resource.

5. Now make a sheet like the first two, only this one will record only your hours at work. Make each horizontal block a half-hour, using sixteen lines to cover an eight-hour day. The next week, record in a word or two how you spent each half-hour. This means you should record at least once every hour what you did in the past two and a half hours while it's fresh in your mind. At the end of this exercise you're really going to get an amazing picture of how you spend your time. We live our lives, not one day at a time, not even an hour at a time, but in three- to ten-minute bursts or events. When we are aware of this, it becomes amazingly apparent how much of our time is either wasted or poorly spent. The goal is not to become so regimented that we effectively utilize every minute of our day but rather to take control and to harness the direction of our minutes and hours to serve our priorities. Most people's lives are controlled by their days. Highly successful people capture the hours and take control of their days. Awareness of your hours and days is the first and most important step.

6. Reviewing your third page, brainstorm as to how you can make better use of the half-hours that you felt were wasted or poorly spent because they did not reflect your heartfelt priorities.

7. Attend a time-management seminar such as Franklin Quest's day-planning system. Franklin Quest's information number is (800) 767-1776.

8. List and clearly detail your other limited resources (money, talents, abilities, knowledge).

9. With that list determine which of those limited resources you want to expand or make the most of. Then determine which ones you can expand on your own and which ones will require the help of others. Once again the purpose of this exercise is to make you aware of your limited resources and gain a vision of how to expand them.

Keys to Stellar Success

Unlocking the Doors to Success in Any Arena, Business or Personal

While locked doors are truly impassable barriers to many, they offer no resistance to those who hold the keys.

Anyone can succeed to a certain degree, but what does it take to achieve higher levels of success than you've ever thought possible? Success for an amateur rocket builder is buying a model rocket, installing a small engine, launching it, and sending it one or two thousand feet in the air. I did that when I was thirteen and loved it, but had our top rocket scientists of the fifties and sixties used that same standard for measuring *their* success, our national defense, our communications industry, our entire world would be radically different.

While this may be obvious, the underlying principle that it illustrates has been lost to countless millions: that success is not an inflexible yardstick by which we measure ourselves. Rather, it's more like a tape measure that keeps lengthening faster than we are growing.

The first and single most critical factor in succeeding is gaining an accurate vision of what true success is for *you!* If you never get a clear picture in your mind of what *you* consider true success, you will miss it—and perhaps you won't even travel in the right direction. What you consider success today is most likely very different from what you considered it to be ten years ago. And what you consider to be success ten years from now will most likely differ from what you consider success today. But we don't live in yesterday or tomorrow, so we must start with a clear vision and definition of what we consider success today.

Identify or define in general terms what you consider success to be for *you*.

All of us have different priorities and desires. As a thirteen-year-old model-rocket builder, my vision of success was a three-stage rocket where all three stages would ignite, propelling the rocket a thousand feet into the air, and the parachute would then open in time to bring the third stage safely back to earth. At the same time, America's top rocket scientist Wernher von Braun's vision of success was building a rocket that would put the first man on the moon and return him safely to earth. While our visions were similar in general terms (we both wanted to launch rockets and bring them safely back to earth), they were vastly different in three ways.

First, they were different in **degree** (my ship had to travel only a thousand feet up and a thousand feet down. Von Braun's ship had to travel 230,000 miles, land on the moon, get back into orbit around the moon, and then travel another 230,000 miles and land safely on earth). So as you can see, visions of success differ first in *degree*. But our visions are also different in terms of personal challenge and ultimate outcome.

In terms of **personal challenge,** achieving my success involved spending a few dollars in a hobby shop, taking a few hours to build the rocket correctly, and spending a few minutes to launch and retrieve it. Achieving von Braun's vision required billions of dollars, millions of man-hours from tens of thousands of people, and finding solutions to thousands of problems that had never been solved before. Achieving his vision required an incredible long mental and physical stretch, while mine required no stretch at all.

In terms of **ultimate outcome,** if I succeeded, I would get a brief thrill, the rocket would be salvaged, and the red ant in the nose cone would live to see another launch. If von Braun succeeded, three crew members would continue to breathe earth's fresh air, and a whole new era of space travel would begin.

So when you begin to write down your general description of what you would consider success for you, start by thinking in terms of ultimate outcome, attaching the degree of success you've envisioned, and then clarify the personal challenge involved. For example, if you're talking in terms of money, do you define the ultimate outcome of your success as $50,000 per year or $1 million per year? If you are talking in terms of a marital relationship, would you define your successful ultimate outcome as "a marriage that isn't an emotional drain" or as "a marriage that is the most fulfilling area in life"? Both are legitimate ultimate outcomes to seek but are significantly different in terms of degree and personal challenge required.

Finally, in general terms, clarify the personal challenge involved in terms of ease or difficulty. If it requires too little effort or stretch on your part, your vision of success in terms of ultimate outcome and degree is too *low.* You need to set your sights higher. If the personal challenge required seems ridiculously impossible, you may have to lower your sights, but don't do that *yet.* Even "impossible" visions are often attainable when you seek to bring them about in a planned, orderly way.

When I was making $7,200 a year in my first job after college, it would have been ridiculous to set my sights at making $2 million a year. Today, if my sights were set at $2 million a year, I'd be looking backward. When did "the impossible" become "the achievable," and when did "the achievable" become a "step backward"? Remember that success isn't a yardstick, it's an ever lengthening tape measure. What may seem impossible to you today can become achievable to you sooner than you think.

Identify and define in detailed, specific terms your visions of success (ultimate outcome, degree, and personal challenge).

Now it's time to get very specific in terms of your vision of success in any area you desire more success. Once again we start with ultimate outcome and degree, and then move into the area of personal challenge. But this time we're going to get painfully specific. If you don't go into this kind of detail, the ultimate outcome you desire and the degree of success you desire will always remain out of reach—a dream or a mirage.

Back to our example of your vision of a successful marital relationship. If you've defined success in this area as "a relationship that isn't an emotional drain," you would now list the *specific* negative attributes about the relationship that make it emotionally draining and the *specific* change to each negative attribute that you think would need to take place for the relationship *not* to be draining.

For example, you might list the the negative attributes you want to change as criticism, complaining, screaming at the kids, and fighting. Next, you would list the specific ultimate outcomes and degrees to which you want each one changed; for example:

1. Instead of constant criticism you would like to receive lots of praise and occasional helpful suggestions.

2. Instead of complaining, you'd like to see appreciation.
3. Instead of screaming at the kids, you would like your mate to correct them with a firm but softer tone of voice.
4. Instead of fighting, you'd like to be able to discuss differences of opinion in a more respectful manner.

Next, list the tasks involved in pursuing these ultimate outcomes; for example:

1. Make personal changes you need to make to be an example to your mate (such as replacing your own criticism of your mate with praise; using softer tones of voice and avoiding accusations to keep arguments from escalating into fights; correcting your kids without expressing anger).
2. Determine what you want to say to your mate on each issue and create a positive way to say it.
3. Assign a time for discussing each issue.

Reconsider your definition and vision for each area of success, evaluating the personal challenge that vision requires.
Starting with your general vision, and then working through each specific item you've written down, ask two questions:
Is the personal challenge great enough to require a stretch mentally, emotionally, spiritually, or physically?
Is meeting the challenge possible, considering the situation and the internal and external resources available?
If your vision of success does not require enough personal challenge to stretch you, there will be little satisfaction or lasting benefit in achieving that success. If that is the case, this is the time to revise your goal *upward*. In our example, instead of defining a successful marital relationship as "one that isn't emotionally draining," you might want to redefine success as "a marital relationship that is emotionally fulfilling." Add to the

lists you made above those attributes or qualities that would transform the relationship from an emotional drain to one that is satisfying and fulfilling.

If, on the other hand, you look at your general vision and your specific lists and the personal challenge requires significant stretching, you need to look at both the general vision and specific lists in terms of the internal and external resources available to you. For example, if you've begged your mate a hundred times to stop criticizing you and the criticisms have only increased, you may deduce that one more request is not likely to change anything. So now you have to consider your vision of that ultimate outcome in light of both the internal and external resources available to you. On the internal side, Do you have the ability to create and use an emotional word picture that would help your mate understand how his or her criticism makes you feel? Or do you have the patience to handle a gradual reduction of criticism?

On the external side, Can you get your mate to visit a marriage counselor with you? Can you get your mate to watch Gary Smalley's "Hidden Keys to Loving Relationships" videos? Or can you recruit the help of friends or family?

Achieving anything significant in life always requires recruiting external resources. Whether it's enlisting the help of a marriage counselor, borrowing from a bank, or gaining wisdom and encouragement from a mentor or partner, achieving maximum success in any area of our life requires outside sources of help. To think you can maximize your success without outside help means your goals are too low or you're not being realistic. Show me anyone in America who has achieved significant success in any area of life, and I'll show you tremendous outside resources that were called on to achieve that success.

If you have reconsidered your vision for success in light of the personal challenge required and the internal and external resources available to you, and determined that achieving it is impossible, don't lower your sights or vision yet. That may ultimately be necessary but not until you have applied the next two keys.

Find, recruit, and utilize the external sources necessary to achieve maximum success in a given area.

If your vision of success seems out of reach in light of the internal and external resources available to you, your next step toward success is to find, recruit, and effectively utilize the external sources that *will* enable you to achieve your vision.

First, you have to identify as many *possible* external sources as you can, in both general and specific terms. So for your marriage, in general terms your list might include the following:

1. Minister or other church counselors
2. Licensed marriage and family therapists
3. Books on marriage or relationships
4. Videotapes on marriage or relationships
5. Other couples that you and your mate respect
6. Mutually respected family members

Once your general list is completed, get specific and write down the names or titles of the external resources that fall into each general category you've listed. This may take a little or a lot of research. For example, there are probably dozens or even hundreds of therapists in your city, but how do you know who the good ones are? That's where the work comes in. Do your homework, whether it's seeking referrals or reading book or tape reviews.

Now that you've identified your possible external resources, you have to recruit their help. If it's a counselor, that means a phone call or a visit; if it's a book, it means a trip to the bookstore. In business, whether you're trying to enlist the help of a banker, a mentor, or a partner, you're going to have to create an effective presentation (oral, written, or both) in order to re-cruit a worthy resource. Strategies and Tips for Creating Irre-sistible Sales Presentations and Ad Campaigns on page 104 gives you the essence of the elements necessary to a good pre-sentation. If you're thinking in terms of recruiting partners or mentors, you should review the "Notebook for Success" sec-tion of Chapters 4 and 5.

Build and use stepladders to climb over walls instead of trying to jump over them.

Perhaps the greatest single deterrent to achieving significant success in any area is viewing the distance between where you are now and where you want to be. If you're on the ground and success is twenty feet high, you might say, "I can't reach that" or think that you could never jump that high. You're right. In fact, there's not a player in the NBA who could jump that high. Even with a pole, the world's greatest pole-vaulter can't get that high.

That being the case, like the vast majority of people, you turn around and walk away from the challenge. You then set your sights on success that is only six feet high. How tragic. For although you could never jump twenty feet in the air, all you needed was two boards twenty feet long, fifteen boards two feet long, a few nails, and a hammer, and the impossible would have become attainable. Significant goals are almost never achieved in a single mighty leap but rather one step at time.

Instead of giving up and lowering your sights to insignificant visions of success, keep your sights high and learn to build stepladders. The wonderful thing about climbing a stepladder is that you only have to take one small step at a time. That's the secret to the success of some of our products, such as Richard Simmons's Deal-A-Meal and "Where There's a Will There's an 'A.'" Deal-A-Meal isn't a crash diet that people can use to achieve their ideal weight in a month, but when used correctly, they lose a little bit of weight each week—one week at a time. After a lot of weeks, they've lost a lot of weight. One man lost over six hundred pounds, and thousands lost over a hundred pounds.

In the same manner, we've seen thousands of students go from D's and F's to straight A's and B's with "Where There's A Will There's an 'A.'"

So how do you build this ladder? First, you must clearly identify where you are right now and where you want to be (your vision of success) as outlined in this chapter. Next, you need to identify the specific intermediate goals that need to be achieved along the way to your destination. Then you must list the specific tasks that need to be completed to achieve each intermediate goal. Finally, you begin the journey by taking the first step, completing the first task.

Back to our marriage example: If the first "intermediate" goal is to reduce your mate's criticism of you, your first task may be to reduce your criticism of your mate. Your next task is to communicate in a way that's clearly understood how your mate's criticism makes you feel and how much it would mean to you if your mate could replace it with encouragement, praise, or help. You begin moving toward your lofty goal of a fulfilling marriage one attainable step after another.

The Bible tells us that the Israelites wandered in the wilderness for forty years before they finally entered the Promised Land. It was only an eleven-day walk from where they began, and yet they took forty years. Why? Because they were told that the land was full of giants who would easily defeat them in battle. So rather than risk losing the battle, they simply gave up and wandered around for forty years. After all that wandering (and a whole generation dying without entering the land that God had given them), they finally obeyed God and entered the land. They easily won every battle, and the very people whom they had feared surrendered without a fight.

Their error is repeated every day by millions who scope out the obstacles to their success and instantly turn and run rather than building stepladders to climb over the obstacles to achieve significant success. Never lower your sights until you've done everything you can to build a ladder.

If you truly cannot build one, your vision of success has flunked the ladder test. *Now* is the time to lower your sights to a more attainable goal.

Periodically review and revise your vision of success.

If success is an ever lengthening tape measure, it's critical that you regularly review your vision, examine where you've come from, where you are, where you want to go, and when you want to get there. In 1976 my vision of success for our company was achieving annual sales of $10 million. In 1988 my vision of success had expanded to $50 million. And by 1994 it had expanded to $200 million. As we achieved and surpassed all those goals, our goals were constantly being revised upward.

By the way, goals and visions of success should always be written down. Even geniuses like Ben Franklin and Thomas Edison never trusted their goals to memory. If they and other successful achievers in history needed to record their visions and goals in writing, how can *we* expect to achieve significant successes without tracking them? Recording your goals, whether on paper or computer disk, magically turns the intangible into the tangible.

Identify, devise, and utilize "creative alternatives."

Persistence doesn't mean that if you run into a wall, you turn around and run into it over and over again. Nor is persistence repeatedly racing a three-legged horse hoping that eventually it will win. For every good idea there are thousands of bad ones, and trying to make a bad idea succeed will not work, no matter how many times you try it. Persistence isn't trying the same thing over and over again until it succeeds; rather, it is trying a multitude of different approaches until you find the right one.

The key element in successfully persisting in the face of obstacles or failure is the ability to identify or devise creative alternatives.

Our first infomercial for the Lori Davis Hair Care line featured Cher as our spokesperson and generated three hundred thousand customers. After one year on the air, however, our response rate had fallen off, and we decided to do a second infomercial featuring the same products with the same celebrity endorser. How could we hope to double the current response we were getting? Going out with a new show offering the same products at the same price with the same endorser would result in no more than a 5 to 10 percent increase, yet we needed an increase of at least 100 percent. We couldn't change the product, we couldn't change the endorser. What could we change? We desperately needed a creative alternative.

The creative alternative I devised was to offer our $40 hair care kit free for a thirty-day trial. If the buyers didn't like the products, they could return them, and their credit card would never be charged. If they kept the products past the thirty days, their credit card would be charged accordingly. The result was more than a doubling of our existing response rate.

Thomas Edison came up with more than 500 creative alternatives before he found one that worked. If he had stopped after 450, we might still be lighting our homes with candles and kerosene. When you reach an obstacle to your success or an attempt to succeed has failed, devise a number of creative alternatives and begin trying them one at a time. Each one that fails makes you a little smarter.

Persist. Like the Energizer bunny, just keep going and going and going.

Like you and me, the vast majority of superachievers have ordinary IQs. What separates them from the crowd isn't their intelligence, it's their persistence. They know more failures, they experience more strikeouts, they suffer greater defeats. But instead of quitting, they just keep coming up to the plate and taking more swings. And the more swings they take, the more times they get on base. And the more times they get on base, the more times they score.

The great news is that this very attribute—the single greatest key to success—is something you can choose to do. If success were dependent on IQ or physical prowess, our success would be beyond our control, and we would be at the mercy of genetics. Fortunately, that is not the case. So if you never enjoy the fruits of significant success, you can't blame your parents and you can't blame your teachers. You can only admit that you set your sights too low or never had the tenacity to persist to the point of achieving significant success.

Notebook for Success

Designing and Achieving Your Game Plan for Success

KEYS TO STELLAR SUCCESS (REVIEW)

Identify or define in general terms what you consider "success" to be for *you*.

Identify and define in detailed, specific terms your visions of success (ultimate outcome, degree, and personal challenge).

Reconsider your definition and vision for each area of "success" evaluating the personal challenge that vision requires.

Find, recruit, and utilize the external sources necessary to achieve maximum success in a given area.

Build and use stepladders to climb over walls instead of trying to jump over them.

Periodically review and revise your vision of success.

Identify, devise, and utilize "creative alternatives."

Persist. Like the Energizer bunny, just keep going and going and going.

PERSONAL INVENTORY FOR SUCCESS

1. Write down a general description of what you consider success to be for you in any individual area. (Think in terms of ultimate outcome, attaching the degree of success you've envisioned.)
2. Clarify the "personal challenge" required to achieve that success, in terms of ease or difficulty: Does it require too little or too much stretch on your part?
3. List specific things from your personal or business life that you want to achieve or change.
4. Looking at the list you made in number 3, write down what you want those items changed to.
5. List the specific tasks required to achieve the ultimate

outcomes and specific changes you've listed above.

6. Assign a specific time for starting and completing each task.

7. Review each task and the general vision above, and determine if there is enough personal challenge to require you to stretch yourself mentally, emotionally, spiritually, or physically, *or* is meeting the challenge impossible in light of the current internal and external resources available to you?

8. List the internal resources you will need to achieve each of your specific tasks or goals. (For example, if you're starting a business, do you need marketing knowledge, design and manufacturing knowledge, financial knowledge, and so forth?)

9. Looking at what's needed to achieve your goals and tasks, if you do not have the needed resources internally, list these as external resources you need to recruit. (For example, if you're great at marketing but have no expertise in design and manufacturing, rather than giving up on your goal, the design and manufacturing expertise goes on your external resource list that you need to identify now and recruit later.)

10. Identify the types of people or specific names of people who can provide each of the external resources you need to recruit.

11. Create a presentation to recruit the people you need to provide your external resources. (See Strategies and Tips for Irresistible Sales Presentations and Ad Campaigns.)

12. Build and use stepladders: Identify where you are right now. Identify where you want to be. List the intermediate goals and steps you need to take. Take the first step.

13. Write down potential creative alternatives you can implement anytime you approach or hit a roadblock.

CHAPTER 14

Why ATC's Success Rate Is 135 Times Greater Than the Industry Average

The Secrets to Our Unparalleled Success Rate and Productivity

Beneath the secrets of ATC's success lie important principles that can be applied to any area of your business or personal life.

INSIGHT 1: ONE MAN'S TREASURE IS ANOTHER MAN'S TRAP!

I recently read an article in one of America's most respected business magazines in which the writer told all Fortune 500 companies that infomercials were the wave of the future and the perfect springboard into successful niche marketing. He went on to say that most Fortune 500 companies had already directed their ad agencies to begin the development of infomercials. This writer was right on one count and wrong on two. He was right that most major companies are currently pursuing infomercial marketing possibilities, but he was wrong to say that every company should look into infomercials, that infomercials represented the perfect springboard into "niche marketing."

Niche marketing is trying to capture a smaller, more specialized segment of a market instead of going after larger, more generic territory. It's a valid marketing strategy. For example, if you were in the magazine business and applied this concept, instead of starting a magazine for athletes in general, you might focus on one for runners. Or an even more directed niche would be to focus specifically on marathoners rather than the larger market of runners in general.

But the concept of using an infomercial for niche marketing is as inefficient and ridiculous as using an F-16 jet fighter to shoot down a flock of geese. You could do it, but what a waste of money! A simple shotgun would be a lot more effective and a lot cheaper. To date, nearly every Fortune 500 company that has entered the infomercial market place has failed miserably.

You're probably wondering: If that's true, why are all these billion-dollar companies (with lots of Harvard MBAs and enormous marketing research budgets) interested in pursuing infomercials? First, they have a misconception of the size of infomercial audiences and the amount of money most infomercial marketers are making. Second, they think that if small companies nobody has ever heard of can succeed, they can, too. And finally, their ad agencies who make their money from producing and distributing the infomercials (even if the infomercials fail) aren't about to try to dissuade their clients from attempting to enter the field. Convincing their clients to try an infomercial puts money *into* their pockets, while not trying takes money *out*.

But major corporations aren't simply the victims of aggressive ad agencies. They are easily persuaded to give infomercials a try because they believe one or more of five common misconceptions:

1. It's a great way to market existing products.
2. Infomercials are a cheap way to take a product to the marketplace.
3. Infomercials are making huge profits for the dozens of companies using them.
4. Infomercials are the perfect way to introduce new products to the marketplace.
5. The infomercial is a great new advertising and marketing medium for major corporations.

These *major* misconceptions are believed by nearly everyone I meet or read about. I therefore feel obligated to set the record straight on each of them as follows:

MISCONCEPTION: **It's a great way to market existing products.**
REALITY: The most successful infomercial marketers (of which there are only a handful) create products specifically designed for infomercial marketing rather than creating an infomercial to sell an existing product. If a company has a product that already has retail distribution (whether through stores, dealers, or a sales force), it's nearly impossible to sell it successfully through an infomercial. For 999 out of 1,000 products, an infomercial is only an expensive trash can to throw lots of money into.

MISCONCEPTION: **Infomercials are a cheap way to take a product to the marketplace.**
REALITY: If you think thirty-second television commercials are expensive, try buying thirty-minute television commercials. Yes, they can be cheaper than buying thirty seconds of prime time, but for the audience size you get, they're a lot more expensive.

When you buy thirty-second spots, the price of the spot is a direct function of the ratings or audience size. Infomercials draw such small audiences, they don't even *get* a rating. Consequently, their price isn't based on audience size (or the stations would be practically giving them away). Instead, their prices are totally arbitrary, determined strictly by whatever a television station can sell the time for. And because there's a lot more demand for infomercial time than there is supply, broadcast stations and cable superstations are able to demand a lot more money for it than the time is really worth.

The price of quality infomercial time has risen more than 300 percent in the past three years. Add to that the fact that audience sizes have dropped almost as dramatically, and you begin to see why 199 out of every 200 infomercials produced fails to make a profit. Many companies that successfully marketed products through infomercials even two years ago wouldn't have a prayer of making money today in light of the high cost of time and the reduced audience sizes.

MISCONCEPTION: **Infomercials are making huge profits for the dozens of companies using them.**

REALITY: When we introduced our first infomercial in 1987, there were only a handful of other companies selling their products using infomercials. Most were out of business within two years. Since that time, many have come and gone. We have always had the good fortune to be the largest and most profitable company in the business. Until this year there were five major companies dominating the marketplace, with dozens of small companies—most of whom get only one product on the air, lose a bunch of money, and then never spill their blood in this arena again.

In 1993, of our four major competitors, the two largest lost over $27 million between them and may not continue to survive much longer. The other two made money, but not much. Fortunately, we had a very good year. At the same time, several Fortune 500 companies, along with one of America's most successful entertainment companies and one of America's largest retailers all tried their hand at infomercials and failed. So no matter what glowing reports you read, no matter what you're told by ad agencies, production companies, or media-buying companies, no matter what you read in the industry trade literature, the water isn't fine. It's very shallow and it's full of dead bodies, so look before you leap.

MISCONCEPTION: **Infomercials are the perfect way to introduce new products to the marketplace.**

REALITY: Infomercials may be a good way to introduce a new product, but they're more likely to be a disastrous way. They are definitely not a perfect way. If you don't believe me, ask Revlon how their Dolly Parton line of makeup did. Infomercials have been a great way for us to introduce new products to the marketplace, and I hope they continue to be, but if television stations and cable channels keep raising the prices of their air time and first-timers keep trusting their media-buying agencies who will pay whatever prices the stations demand, even *our* best efforts won't be able to launch new products successfully through infomercials.

MISCONCEPTION: **The infomercial is a great new advertising and marketing medium for major corporations.**

REALITY: Without a doubt this is the most damaging misconception of all. As I said in the beginning of this chapter, countless Fortune 500 companies are developing infomercials. Once those infomercials have been produced, they need to be broadcast. The ad agencies and media-buying companies often go out and pay "whatever it takes" to get that infomercial on the air. As a result, they drive up the cost of the time, not only for themselves but for the entire industry. By the time they figure out that their infomercial has failed, the damage is already done. But for every company that tries and fails, there are five more standing in line to step up to the plate and take their swings. The result is ever rising prices that may ultimately make infomercials a thing of the past. By continually raising their prices and catering to the ignorance of the first-timers, the television stations and cable superstations are killing the geese that lay the golden eggs.

These five misconceptions are the primary reasons 99.5 percent of everyone else's infomercials fail to make a profit. Companies are fooled into believing that infomercials are a viable marketing avenue for their products. At today's prices and audience levels, infomercials represent a viable marketing channel for only a very select number of products, and that number continues to diminish with each price hike of TV time.

Why does any of this matter to you if you're not interested in infomercial marketing? Most of my readers are, I hope, reading this book to improve their chances of success in areas other than infomercials. If that is the case with you, you may be wondering what the value is of what you've just read. The value is the first insight of this chapter: One man's treasure is another man's trap. Just because you see someone else making a lot of money in a given area, don't assume that particular area holds a pot of gold for you.

The first people to enter any business or industry usually find it a lot easier to succeed than those who enter later. Success is rarely found where the crowd has gathered. A crowded field doesn't mean there's a pot of gold for everyone; more likely it means there is not enough food and a lot of litter to pick up.

Why is ATC's success rate 135 times greater than the industry average? Having just painted such a gloomy (but accurate) picture of our industry, I should now focus on this question that must occasionally cross the minds of our competitors. But before I go on, maybe I should explain what I mean by success rate. I'm referring to the percentage of infomercials produced that are actually rolled out nationally *and* make a profit. One out of fifteen produced get rolled out nationally, and one out of thirteen of those end up making a profit. Thus the "success rate" for our industry is about one out of every two hundred, or .5 percent. To date I've produced twenty-four, and twenty have been rolled out (83 percent); all of those have made millions of dollars in profit. But true success by our definition is not just the percentage of infomercials we produce that roll out and make millions of dollars in profits, there are three other important factors: customer satisfaction, production and product quality, and the lack of significant legal and regulatory problems. We not only lead the industry in the first category, but we also believe we lead it in all three. Our success is not due to any single factor but to the following ten.

1. An unparalleled partnership in terms of commitment, motivation, talent, and division of labor—in that order.

If you've read my previous chapters (and haven't just skipped ahead to this one), you already know that this is by far the number one reason for our success. This most important element in our success started at the top with Bob Marsh. He was totally committed to each of the seven other partners, and we were motivated by his love to perform at levels way above our known abilities and capacities. That commitment and motivation gave us the necessary time and persistence to develop various talents in our industry that are seemingly light-years ahead of competition.

Think about it: How many companies have a direct-response television team that has remained together for twenty years, from the days when the longest commercials were two minutes and telephone orders were taken by hand instead of on computers. We have been together since the early days, and we've pioneered most of the breakthroughs and formulas that the rest of the industry has tried to copy.

I say this not to boast but simply to give an insight as to why we have achieved radically different results from our competitors. First and foremost, it's the team. It's each partner having his own area of expertise and having had twenty years to experiment, fail, and succeed over and over again, ultimately becoming the absolute best at what he does. Today, as we train those who will someday take our places, they are gaining in a relatively short period of time the expertise that took us the better part of our adult lives to learn.

2. Our business and marketing philosophy

For many people, a corporate philosophy is something they print in their annual report or hang on their wall. With us it was the very foundation of our business even though it was never spoken, much less written down. Once again, it started at the top with Bob Marsh and trickled down to each of us and into every area of our business. Our entire philosophy could be summed up in a single word: Honor. We treat everyone we deal with—our employees, vendors, viewers, and ultimately our customers—with respect. This may sound clichéd or altruistic, but for us it is a daily reality—where the rubber meets the road. No, we don't honor all the people every day every time we deal with them. We blow it regularly, but we really try!

And it makes an incredible difference. We are proud of all our products and their quality, and because we offer the best products we can, I believe in every one of them. And because I believe in them, I can usually sell them in record numbers.

3. Direct-response two-minute history

Another key factor in our success rate is our twenty-year history in using two-minute direct-response television commercials. Needless to say, this is another factor that would be hard for any of our competitors to duplicate. Before I had ever written and produced my first thirty-minute infomercial, I had written and produced over eight hundred two-minute commercials selling dozens of various products and services. With each commercial I wrote and produced I had the opportunity to test prices, offers, script elements, celebrity endorsements, and on and on.

Each test brought new insights as to what worked and what didn't. The process of testing over eight hundred commercials in twelve years could make anyone smart—even me! How ridiculous to think that any company (no matter how big) can come in and hit home runs without having had years of practice. Sure they might get lucky and have the bat in the right place at the right moment *once,* but watch them when they come up to the plate a second, third, and fourth time.

4. Product selection: half science, half gut feel

I learned in our two-minute days that no matter how great a product may be, it can still fail in direct-response TV. I also learned that far more products will fail than will succeed. The sad thing is that everyone who has invented a product has thought that TV was the perfect way to introduce it. Most products are defeated by the math alone; that is, the spread between the cost to manufacture the product and the price the consumer is willing to pay for it is too narrow to pay for the high cost of the TV time. For example, if something costs $8 to manufacture and the perceived value is only $19.95, the spread is not nearly enough to cover the cost of the TV time. I would guess that this factor alone disqualifies about ninety out of every one hundred products that people bring to us.

The second greatest disqualifying factor is the size of the market for the product. In most cases, for a product to be successful on TV, it must appeal to a large segment of the viewers you can reach in the time periods you can afford to run in. For example, if you have a product that appeals only to men, its chances of success are minimal. That's because it's hard to reach men during the less expensive times of day (daytime, early morning, late night). If you have a product for new mothers, they represent only a small part of any viewing audience, so that product likewise would have only a small chance for success.

The third major disqualifying factor is the product's lack of uniqueness and strong appeal. It may be a terrific product, but if similar products are available in stores, the chances of getting people to order your product from a commercial are slim to none.

After having tested dozens and dozens of products and offers over the years, we have developed a pretty good gut feel for what has a chance of working and what doesn't. In evaluating the direct-response potential of a product, here are some of the major factors I look for.

Does the math work? Is the perceived value for the product a lot higher than the manufactured cost? Ideally, I would like at least a six-to-one ratio. That means if something has a perceived value of $18, I need to be able to get it into my warehouse, manufactured, and packaged for no more than $3. We have had a few successful products where the ratio has been less, but most have had a six-to-one or better.

How wide is the market or universe? There are roughly 100 million TV households in America. When looking at a potential product, one of the first questions you have to explore is how many potential TV households that product will appeal to. For example, I produced two infomercials featuring Frank and Kathie Lee Gifford as our celebrity endorsers. One of these infomercials offered a video series on relationships, "Hidden Keys to Loving Relationships." The other infomercial featured a video series for parents of preadolescent children. It was titled "Teaching Your Children Values for Life." While the potential universe for the relationship tapes was probably 90 million households, the potential universe for the parenting video series was approximately 15 million. While such a limited universe would normally discourage us from even considering such a product, we decided to give it a try.

Our reasoning was that even though the universe or market for parenting tapes was much smaller, values had become a hot topic. We felt that the universe (which was one-sixth the size of the other universe) was likely to be a far more *responsive* one. In other words, while we might get a response rate of two orders per thousand from the larger relationships universe, we might get a response rate of eight or ten per thousand from the parenting universe. This is a rare case in which a smaller universe did not keep us from going forward on a product.

How unique is the product? While this factor should be an obvious consideration for any infomercial marketer, I am continually amazed at how many infomercials I see on the air offering products that aren't that different from what is already available to consumers through other avenues. Needless to say, those infomercials are usually not on the air for long. Given the choice of buying the same product from a retail store or a television offer, the vast majority of consumers will always opt for the store. If a product offered in an infomercial is not obviously unique in features, benefits, or price from what is already available in retail stores, the product has almost no chance of succeeding.

How strong are the hooks? Another extremely important factor in my selection of a product is the strength of the emotional or demonstrative hooks that distinguish it from any other product. One of the main reasons I wanted to test the parenting video series was that even though the universe was small, the hooks in the product were extremely compelling. What parents aren't afraid of the influences of the media on their children? Look at a few of the statistics that I discovered when I was searching for the emotional hooks for this product.

- 72 percent of today's teens have had sexual intercourse by the time they graduate from high school.
- Of these, 25 percent have had intercourse with at least four partners.
- 25 percent of all high school graduates have a sexually transmitted disease.
- 30 percent of all high school seniors report they've been drunk within the last month.
- 85 percent of today's high school juniors and seniors admit they cheat on exams.

How many parents of young children do you know who want their kids to become a part of statistics like these? These are the kinds of hooks that persuaded me to pursue this project in spite of its relatively small potential universe.

How demonstrable is the product or its benefits? When it comes to selling a product through an infomercial, nothing beats a good demonstration. Now when we think of demonstrations, everyone thinks of a mechanical demonstration such as showing the unique features of a kitchen appliance or a piece of exercise equipment. But don't forget "before" and "after" pictures or testimonials. We were able to launch one of the fastest-growing cosmetic companies in America and the fastest-growing hair care lines—and in both cases the demonstration was the before and after makeovers and testimonials. If a product's uniqueness can't be shown in some kind of demonstration, the chances of it succeeding in an infomercial are greatly reduced.

How much greater will the perceived value be than the price I offer? If the perceived value of a product is $100 and you can't afford to sell it for significantly less than that perceived value, it doesn't have much a chance of succeeding in an infomercial format. For example, the perceived value of the cosmetic kit we sell in our Victoria Jackson infomercial is over $200 when compared to comparable department-store-quality cosmetics. Our price for the same items of what we consider to be better quality is $90. And because we were able to demonstrate the comparative value, we were able to sell our cosmetics very successfully through our infomercials. The greater the spread between the legitimate perceived value and the offering price, the better the chance of success.

While these six factors are key in determining which products we select for testing, product selection itself—a key factor to our successful track record—is only one of ten critical factors to our success.

5. Celebrity Selection

The fifth critical factor for our success has been our ability to match the right celebrity to the right product, and our willingness to pay good celebrities the kind of money they are worth. Without the ability to make good celebrity-product matches, and without a willingness to pay them what they are worth, our company would never have even made it past the launch phase in 1976, much less achieved the enormous success of the past twenty years. This factor has been so instrumental in our success that I spent a whole chapter telling about it (Chapter 8).

6. Writing honest infomercials with class, that sell

Writing . . . even if you have the best new product ever created, if you can't write a good thirty-minute script, you can end up striking out. Fortunately for me, I had twelve years and seven hundred commercials in which to learn how to write scripts that sell before I ever wrote my first infomercial. These were all two-minute commercials, so I had to learn how to make the sale in two minutes, which is infinitely more difficult than making a sale in thirty minutes. Imagine spending twelve years having to win mile races with times under four minutes, and then entering mile races where you could win as long as your time was under eight minutes. How often could you beat your competition when most of them had never even *walked* a mile, much less run one?

Honest infomercials . . . If you've spent a lot of time watching infomercials over the years, these two terms may seem contradictory. So many of them seem to make wild, exaggerated claims. Our conscience and our desire to have long-term relationships with our customers kept us out of the quick-buck infomercials from which many of our early competitors got temporarily rich. You don't have to make dishonest or wildly exaggerated claims—or, for that matter, even mildly exaggerated claims—when you're selling a great product at a fair price. You don't have to yell and shout and scream and show bogus demonstrations. If you have a product that isn't really all it appears to be, you may have to resort to dishonest claims to sell it, but I'm very thankful that the people in our company, such as Jim Shaughnessy, John Marsh, Patty Brenner, and Brett Smiley, not to mention the authors, inventors, and innovators we work with, hand me great products that never need to be hyped to be sold.

With Class . . . Because we have great products, we don't have to resort to carnival or boardwalk sales tactics, and we are able to write classy, intelligent infomercials that treat our viewers and customers with respect. If our productions weren't created with class, we would never be able to attract major celebrities. And without our major celebrities, our business would have failed years ago.

That sell . . . Many of our competitors have proved it's easy to produce incredibly creative and beautiful infomercials that don't sell. The best example of this is the "dramatic" format, which has become popular during the past couple of years, in which the presentation centers on a story. They're somewhat entertaining, they're beautifully shot, they win awards, but what a waste of money—and, in some cases, the opportunity to sell a good product. Yes, a few have been slightly to moderately successful, but I am convinced that had those same infomercials used a different format, their success would have been greatly multiplied. We, too, have focused on trying to write and produce infomercials with high creative and production values, but we have kept the selling elements of the infomercial at center stage. I have focused on using television to sell products, and the day I sacrifice making the sale to the ego trip of creating a beautiful, dramatic television masterpiece is the day our company's sales will begin to vaporize.

7. Infomercial production

The seventh critical factor in our success has been our ability to produce believable, great-looking great-selling infomercials at affordable costs. I believe our production team is totally unparalleled in every arena. A writer's greatest disappointment is a production that turns out to be far less than his original vision for the script. In my case, I have the privilege of directing all my productions, but Frank Kovacs is my producer and for fifteen years has been unbelievable in his ability to create productions that not only fulfill my original vision but vastly exceed it *every time*. Our productions aren't cheap, but I'm convinced that Frank gets higher production values for the dollar than any producer in Hollywood.

8. Budgets

Another key factor in our success has been my partners' willingness to give me the production and talent budgets necessary to turn my visions and scripts into reality. For the most part, we spend far more per infomercial than any of our competitors, and fortunately we get what we pay for. No matter how good a script is, if you don't have the budget to turn it into a reality, it's not worth the paper it's written on. Depending on the infomercial, we have spent anywhere from $350,000 to $1.7 million, not including the celebrity fees. Needless to say, if we hadn't hit home runs with a high percentage of those, we would have been out of business a long time ago. For twenty years my partners have sent me out on good faith, never giving me a limitation on what I could spend. But at the same time, knowing my nature, they are sure I won't spend a penny more than I think is absolutely necessary.

9. No outside pressure to sacrifice what's best for our long-term business on the altar of what's expedient.

Many of our competitors are public companies, but we are fortunate to remain privately held. We have therefore never felt outside pressure to produce short-term results that look good on quarterly reports but are often to the long-term detriment of a business. And because every dime we spend or risk is our own, we've always been able to do what is best for our long-term business even if it meant a flat or negative quarter. Some of our most successful programs have required us to go deep into the red for anywhere from a couple of quarters to as long as three years before turning the corner and producing significant profits. Being able to put our long-term interests above short-term appearances has been critical to our business-building efforts and have become the cornerstone of our company.

10. Divine grace

Whether you believe in God or not, the judgment of all the partners in our company is that much of our inspiration, our vision, and all the miraculous events that came our way just in the nick of time at different points in our business came because of the undeserved, unmerited intervention of a kind and loving God. We did nothing that could have earned or deserved the success that started our company, saved our company during the hard times, and set our company on its current track of success. Not only have the miraculous events in our business built our faith along the way, but our faith has also made the ride an exciting and wonderful one.

One Final Question: What Do You Want?

If your goal is to have more success in virtually any area of your life, the principles revealed in this book are guaranteed to equip you with the knowledge you need to achieve a higher degree of success than would otherwise have been possible. Knowledge in itself is not enough, however. The world is full of knowledgeable people whose success never goes past mediocrity. Those who achieve stellar success in any area of life are those who are able to transform knowledge into specific steps of action and then have the decisiveness, courage, and persistence to take those steps. If you wish to raise your level of success from the ordinary to the extraordinary, you must take some very specific steps to apply the knowledge you've gained from this book to your situation. Those steps are carefully detailed and outlined in the Personal Inventory sections at the end of each chapter.

As you begin to apply them, you will see your success rate slowly begin to accelerate, much like a rocket at its liftoff from the launching pad. But the higher you get, the faster you'll accelerate until you finally break loose from the gravitational pull of ordinary achievement. At that point, stellar success will become your everyday experience rather than a once-in-a-lifetime hope or dream.

As you begin to achieve the success that has eluded you, whether in your personal or your professional life, drop me a line at American Telecast, 1230 American Boulevard, West Chester, PA 19382, and tell me what's happening. I'd love to include some of your success stories in my next book or in my videos or newsletters. Also, if you'd like to receive free information on any of my current or future projects, send me your name, address, and telephone number (if you like) or call (800) 641-2999 and ask to be put on Steve Scott's mailing list. It's free, and I will keep you posted on new material I'm working on. I hope that you will achieve success far beyond anything you've ever imagined. I promise: It is not only possible, it's *doable!*

Appendix

Incorporating Critical Elements into a Script

The following scripts show how the critical elements out-lined in Chapter 11 are incorporated into a two-minute spot and into the most successful infomercial in the history of the industry. In its first five months on the air, this in-fomercial sold more three hundred thousand treadmills, totaling over $145 million in sales.

Two-Minute Commercial Script

Boldface copy is Jane's voice over product demo shots.

JANE FONDA Hi, I'm Jane Fonda. Are you in the kind of shape you *want* to be? Would you like to lose weight and keep it off? It takes more than a diet to do that. It takes fat-burning exercise. Not a lot, only a few minutes each day. And that brings me to what I think is the most exciting piece of fitness equipment to come along in a long time. **It's my Walk to the Music Fitness Tread. And it's unlike any treadmill you've ever seen.**

First, there's no intimidating motor or complicated pro-gramming to fool around with. It has a unique horizontal

flywheel that keeps the tread moving smoothly while you're walking. And because there's no motor, you're in complete control. It follows your pace, not vice versa. And because it's at the optimum angle of incline, you burn up to 31 percent more calories than you would walking at a faster speed on a flat surface.

Best of all, it doesn't cost a fortune. And because there's no motor, it comes with a warranty twice as long as some motorized models costing ten times as much.

It comes fully assembled. Just lift up the handles, pop in a "Walk to the Music" musical tape, and start walking. The music will guide you through your level of exercise, whether you're a beginner, intermediate, or advanced. When you're done exercising, fold down the arms and put it away. It's that easy!

Most important, you don't have to risk a dime to try it. Use it for a full thirty days, and if it doesn't give you the best, most enjoyable workout you've ever had, you can return it for a full refund. With its low price and wonderful convenience, you have no excuse for staying out of shape. You can start getting fit the day it arrives! Here's how to order. . . .

Thirty-Minute Infomercial Script
I. Opening

JANE FONDA: Hi, I'm Jane Fonda. And If you're one of the fifty million Americans who's currently dieting to lose weight or one of the millions more who have given up, then I've got some *bad* news . . . and . . . I've got some *great* news! The bad news is, according to *Consumer Reports,* the vast majority of Americans who lose weight by dieting gain it back within two years. Their survey of over ninety-five thousand Americans included all the major dieting programs, including meal replacement shakes and even the more expensive programs that included counseling and special foods. They reported that even the most optimistic weight-control professionals admitted that traditional dieting—cutting calories to lose weight—rarely works in the long term.

But before you get *too* discouraged, let me tell you the *great* news. In the next thirty minutes you're going to learn about what I consider to be two important new developments in fitness that can make it easier not only to lose weight but actually *increase* the fat burning enzymes in your cells and *raise* your metabolism so that your body will burn more calories, ultimately reducing your body fat! All this with less effort than you may think and without spending a fortune.

In a few moments I'm going to introduce my workout class to some of the fitness experts who have been instrumental in these developments. So if you or any member of your family wants to lose weight or simply become a *lot* more fit, stay with us for some of the best news your body will ever hear!

II. Title Sequence: Fitness Breakthroughs of the Nineties

III. Jane seated with LaJean in front of her workout class, with a white board on a stand off to her left.

JANE (to camera): Welcome to our class. But today we're not going to do any aerobic dancing. In fact, we're not going to work out at all. Instead, I'm going to introduce you and our class to a breakthrough that our fitness team has been working on for a long time, something I believe will make it a lot easier, safer, and less expensive to lose weight and get fit.

This is Dr. Lawson, a university professor with a Ph.D. in exercise science and a very valued member of our research team.

LaJean, thanks for joining us.

LAJEAN: My pleasure.

JANE: Before we talk about the latest developments in fitness, I want give our class and our viewers a little quiz about fitness. Question number one:

[voiceover graphic]

The heart-disease risk factor that affects the greatest number of American adults is:

- Smoking
- High cholesterol
- High blood pressure, or
- Insufficient exercise.

[on camera]

The answer is insufficient exercise. In fact, it affects more Americans than the other three risk factors *combined!* It causes over **250,000** deaths each year.

Number 2.

[voiceover graphic]

True or false: With our increased awareness of fitness, *more* Americans are fit *today* then ever?

[on camera]

False. According to the Centers for Disease Control, only twenty-two out of every hundred Americans get a sufficient amount of exercise to maintain good health. That means seventy-eight out of every one hundred *don't* get enough exercise!

Number 3.

[voiceover graphic]

True or false: Even though the vast majority of adults don't get adequate amounts of exercise, kids and teens do.

[on camera]

False. Since the early 1960s there's been a 54 percent increase in obesity among children ages six to eleven. And only 37 percent of today's high schoolers get the exercise they need. Does it matter? Listen to this: Forty percent of all American children have at least one heart-risk factor by the age of twelve. Forty percent! Tragically, we're not only a nation of unfit adults, we're a nation of unfit children.

Number 4.

[voiceover graphic]

The right amount of the right type of exercise always results in which of the following benefits?

- An increase in fat-burning enzymes
- The burning of more fat calories even when you're resting
- Reduction in body fat
- Improved cardiovascular and general health
- All of the above

[on camera]

The answer is all of the above. Now think about it. The right amount of the right kind of exercise gives you all of these tremendous benefits that enable you to feel better, look better, enjoy life more—right now and a lot more as you grow older.

So why do the vast majority of Americans, 78 percent, fail to exercise sufficiently?

Finally, true or false:

[voiceover graphic]

To get the fitness benefits of exercise, you must exercise at your target heart rate for at least twenty to thirty minutes at a time, five or more days a week.

[on camera]

The answer is false. You *don't* need to exercise for twenty or thirty minutes at a time! That's one of the recent major discoveries published by medical researchers at Stanford University and the world-renowned Cooper Clinic. Their discovery makes getting the exercise we need a lot easier.

JANE: Now I'd like to ask each of you in the class—and you at home—what are the main things that keep you from a regular exercise routine? LaJean, let's make a list of these exercise blockers. Would you mind writing them on the board?

LAJEAN: Not at all.

JANE: Sue?

SUE: Time. It's just too hard to carve out an hour a day. Not only the time it takes to exercise, but the time it takes to get to the health club.

JANE: (while LaJean writes TIME on the grease board): Yeah. Time is the number one hurdle that stops most people

OTHER VOICE: Inconvenience. Between work and the kids, there's no way I can consistently carve out a regular time to exercise.

OTHER VOICE: Or you have to drive to a track or health club or exercise outside. And hot, cold, rain, or snow can kill that.

OTHER VOICE: Too tired. The only time I have the hour I need to exercise is at the end of the day, and I'm just too tired.

OTHER VOICE: Boring. I used to go to the health club, but frankly, after twenty minutes of exercise, I get bored.

OTHER VOICE: Too expensive. I can't afford to go to a health club, and I certainly can't afford five hundred or a thousand dollars for a piece of equipment.

OTHER VOICE: I always stop after a few months and the weight comes right back.

OTHER VOICE: I'll be honest: I hate exercise. It's too hard. I get exhausted.

OTHER VOICE: I feel like a klutz. I'm not sure what to do, how to do it, and I'm afraid if I don't do it right, I'll either end up very sore or even injured.

JANE: Well, believe it or not, you're all in for a wonderful surprise because what we're about to show you solves all of those problems—all of them! Without a doubt the biggest obstacle for most of us is time.

LAJEAN: Well, studies show that time is the number one problem for nearly everyone. And the Stanford University study seems to offer a big part of the solution.

We used to teach that to get the fitness benefits of exercise, you needed to exercise at an intensity level of 60 to 80 percent of your maximum heart rate for at least twenty to sixty minutes per session. The Stanford studies showed that that simply is not true. They showed that you get roughly the same benefits from multiple short bouts of exercise that you would get from a single longer bout.

That means that instead of having to carve out twenty or thirty minutes at a time, which as you can see stops most people from an exercise program, you only need to carve out ten minutes at a time, two or three times a day. And all of us can find two or three ten-minute breaks between the time we wake up and the time we go to bed.

VOICE: Yeah, but it takes more than ten minutes if you have to drive to a track or health club.

JANE: And that brings us to our exciting breakthrough! In my opinion it's the most innovative, user-friendly, affordable, and really fun piece of fitness equipment I've ever used. Something that will enable you to overcome every obstacle we've talked about that keeps you and your family from an effective, consistent exercise routine.

It's our "Walk to the Music Fitness Tread," and as you're about to see, it's unlike any other treadmill on the market today.

LaJean, why don't you start with the things that you think separate this unit from the other treadmills on the market.

LAJEAN: *(points to make in her own words)*
    No motor—advantages
    Walk to the music—advantages
    Permanent incline—advantages
    Responsiveness of tread
    Portability
    Durability
    Fully assembled
    No maintenance
    Electronics
    Warranty
    Affordability—price
    Audiotape
    Videotape

JANE: We're going to take a break so you can find out how you can get your family walking to the beat. LaJean, thanks for joining us. We'll be right back.

IV. Interior Spot No. 1

MARY KATE: Jane Fonda's "Walk to the Music" Fitness Tread is unlike any treadmill you've ever seen.

(voice over product demo)

Its unique, high-performance engineering has resulted in a treadmill that is so easy to use and gives such a personal and effective workout, it doesn't need an expensive cumbersome motor or complicated electronics.

It comes fully pre-assembled. Just lift the handrails, tighten two knobs, and you're ready to go. There's nothing intimidating about this unit. You'll never have to step on or off a moving belt. You can start as slowly as you like and then walk at whatever speed is comfortable. And you can change the intensity of your workout as often as you like because the tread moves at your pace, not vice versa. You're in total control.

And because it's at a permanent incline, you'll burn up to 30 percent more calories than you would with *no* incline. You'll also more effectively work your hips, thighs, and buttocks, helping to tone those areas we usually worry about the most.

The digital readout tells you your speed and the time and distance you've walked. And look at this, inside the built-in cassette player is your first "Walk to the Music" workout cassette with individual workouts for beginner, intermediate, and advanced levels. And because you're walking to the beat of music you love, your workouts seem shorter and less intense than they really are. And because there's no motor, there's no maintanence. And you don't have to worry about your children "turning it on" when you're not around. And look at this: When you're finished using it, it's so light and portable, you can easily store it anywhere.

Best of all it's so low-priced, nearly every family can afford it. It even has *double* the warranty of some treadmills costing *ten* times as much. What does that tell you about quality?

And if you order now, you'll also receive this video from Jane, showing you how to make the most of your workouts.

(Mary Kate on camera)

Use it for thirty days, and if you don't love it as much as we do, you can return it for a full refund. But believe me, once you've walked to the music on *this* treadmill, you'll never send it back. Here's how to order. . . .

V. *Back to Show*

JANE: And now I'd like to introduce our second expert. This is Doug Allen. Doug did all the diagnostic and clinical testing on this unit. He's a member of the American College of Sports Medicine, has been a consultant to nearly every major fitness equipment manufacturer in America, and is currently working on projects with Nike and Spaulding, to name a few. Doug, thanks for joining us.

DOUG: I'm glad to be here.

JANE: Tell us the results of your tests.

DOUG: We've tested over forty-five subjects ranging in age from eighteen to seventy-five. And the results were unbelievable. In fact, we recently taped some of the comments from a few of our test participants.

JANE: Let's take a look.

VII. *Portland Testimonials*
(on-camera testimonials for Portland product tests)

VIII. *Back to Jane*

JANE (Reacts to tape and then asks Doug): Now, you've been a consultant to some of the biggest companies in the sports and fitness industries, and as an industry expert, tell me what you think about the Fitness Tread.

[Doug discusses everything he likes about it.]

JANE: I know some of you have to have questions, but while we're answering them, why don't we let some of you try it out. Who wants to be first?

[Calls out three names; they come up, put the headsets on. Doug, Jane, and LaJean get them started and start taking questions.]

[Jane points to raised hand.]

QUESTION: Do you think treadmills are better than rowers, skiers, or cycles?

ANSWER: (Unscripted, spontaneous response.)

QUESTION: Have you compared this to motorized treadmills, and if so how, does it stack up?

ANSWER: (Unscripted, spontaneous response.)

QUESTION: If a motor isn't a big advantage, why do all the expensive treadmills have motors?

ANSWER: (Unscripted, spontaneous response.)

QUESTION: Do you lose anything because you can't swing your arms?

ANSWER: (Unscripted, spontaneous response.)

QUESTION: How much instruction do I need?

ANSWER: (Unscripted, spontaneous response.)

QUESTION: I've seen other non-motorized treadmills in catalogues and on TV. Have you compared these to this unit?

ANSWER: (Unscripted, spontaneous response.)

QUESTION: How do I know that the tape I get with the unit will give me the level of workout I need? Could it be too easy or too hard?

ANSWER: (Unscripted, spontaneous response.)

QUESTION: I've started exercise programs before, but they've never lasted.

ANSWER: (Unscripted, spontaneous response.)

JANE: We took three of our treadmills to [a sports club in Los Angeles]. This outstanding multimillion-dollar facility has the finest equipment money can buy. We placed three "Walk to the Music Fitness" treads next to their $6,500 treadmills and asked their members to compare their workout on our unit to the more expensive ones they normally use. Here's what they said.

IX. Sports Club Testimonials
X. Spot II.

Interior Spot No. 2
(same as Spot No. 1)

XI. JANE [closing]: Well, we're just about out of time. Every year insufficient exercise costs the lives of 250,000 Americans.

Only twenty-two out of every one hundred American adults get enough exercise to gain the fat-burning and health benefits of exercise. You know you need to do something about it, not only for yourself but if you have a family, for their sakes as well. Set an example. All it takes is a small amount of the right kind of exercise.

I'm fifty-five years old, and I feel better today at fifty-five than I did at twenty-five. And you'd better believe that. I want to look and feel as good at sixty-five as I do today. And *exercise is the key*. I'm not up for the strenuous hours of exercise I used to do, but thanks to recent discoveries by medical researchers that we've just discussed, I realize I don't have to.

In a recent issue of *Better Homes and Gardens* an article on home exercise equipment stated, "One of the safest ways to walk, jog, or run is indoors on a treadmill. . . . Leading cardiologists have found that walking briskly on an incline is just about the best exercise you can do."

Now that we know that long, exhausting workout sessions are not necessary to get fit, and now that we've created a quality machine that nearly every family can afford, there's simply no excuse for any man or woman not to get fit. If you're ever going to get into shape, you've got to start sometime. Why not start right now. Just give it a try. I promise, you won't be sorry. Thanks for joining us.

About the Author

Steven K. Scott is a cofounder of the American Telecast Corporation and its group of consumer-goods companies. In addition to creating ATC's marketing programs, he has written and directed more than eight hundred television commercials and twenty-four infomercials selling ATC's product lines. Cher, Jane Fonda, Kathie Lee Gifford, Charlton Heston, Tom Selleck, and Michael Landon are a few of the more than seventy celebrities who have appeared in Steve's commercials and infomercials.

To date, his campaigns have sold more than one billion dollars' worth of products to more than twenty million consumers. In addition to cofounding and building more than a dozen multimillion-dollar companies from the ground up, Steve has also coauthored two best-selling books with Gary Smalley and coproduced nine best-selling videos.